Winning Management Buy-In

Convincing the King That He is Not Invincible to Dragons

By SA Hale and Terry Hale

August 2017

DEDICATION
To our friends, family, and loved ones
Past - Present - Future

Prologue:

How do we as professional engineers and scientists plead our case to vice presidents, senior management, and stakeholders that issues like cybersecurity are real and imminent dangers - "convince the king that he is not invisible to dragons?"

Our text will make use of real world examples from senior management decisions, and we will reinforce these examples with Cognitive Biases, Problem-Solving, Conflict Resolution, Decision Making, Social Engineering tools, tricks, and tips.

In synopsis, our goal is to explain that it is the engineers and scientists who must learn to speak the business language of senior management.

We would like to thank David Downs, Margie Langston, Lorain Phillip, and Chris Stanford for taking the time to review our pre-published manuscript. No, we didn't follow all of your tips and recommendations. We have our own way of doing things incorrectly, but we do appreciate your guidances.

Keywords: Cyber Security, Information Security, Decision Making, Problem Solving, Conflict Resolution, Cognitive Biases, Social Engineering, Communication, Business Psychology, Sales, Marketing.

Table of Content

DISCLAIMER
The contents of this book, detailed presentations and workshops are the results of our research, life experiences, and opinions.

Introduction:

Senior Management buy-in to technical issues is a major requirement for the success of our new endeavors.

The following example will use cyber security breaches as an illusion for the necessity for management buy-in. These breaches have become a familiar story in the daily news. Unfortunately, these stories don't tell the whole narrative. Data loss is happening every day. Some companies own up to the issue quickly while other entities choose to keep these cyber attacks quiet and hide the fact that sensitive information has fallen into the hands of those who shouldn't have access. Either way, this type of news is at least a major headache for the company and can quite quickly turn into a messy financial situation and a loss of both investor and customer confidence.

Security is an example of a Negative Sell

For years there has been this tendency to understate the impact when an incident occurs. However, being proactive to prevent an incident from taking place in the first place is a better approach. We are at a juncture in the technology evolution where processive thinking is beginning to consider prevention as a complement to existing mitigation or detection measures. Are we nearing the end of the "Ostrich effect" to cyber security and technical innovation? Read further in the book for a definition.

The most important aspect of approaching cyber security or technological innovation is management buy-in. The decision makers must have an understanding of the importance of your innovation, cyber, security, technology, etc. program. Without the support of management, it becomes very challenging to make the transition from a reactive stance to a proactive stance. Once the buy-in is accomplished, the responsibility falls on the experts. Detection and mitigation are still critical, but the ultimate goal is to forestall attacks before damage is done proactively.

The key to a good cyber security foundation is to introduce policies and procedures that mandate secure security practices. The policies, of course, should address common avenues of attack such as weak password policies, unauthorized media, and failure to limit

Internet access and control how and for what people use the Internet. In addition, there should have written procedures in place to help our users to understand, learn, and grow with the policies of the organization.

Once all the groundwork has been laid, it is important to implement and maintain the essential infrastructure that makes up a good data science, cyber-security, or any other science-engineering-technology posture. There are many aspects of developing and maintain such an attitude. To meet the ever-growing cyber-security proactive position, numerous aspects of security have to be developed, maintained, and improved as time goes on. If this is not done, then the company will quickly revert to the mitigation stance. The primary approach to dealing with a problem after the damage has occurred has been mitigation. While mitigation is an important position to have,

I hate when it's dark and my brain is like, "Hey, you know what we haven't thought about in a while? Monsters."

it's like closing the barn door after the horse got out. Organizations have to learn to take a precautionary approach to detect attacks and stop the damage before it happens.

Perhaps, the image on the previous page sums up how you feel when it's time to present information to senior management. You look down at your shoes. They ask what time it is, and you go on a tangent telling them how the watch was made.

The goal of this book is to help fellow Geeks learn how to present to senior managers and decision makers, how to market and sell a security solution to them, how to use both Cognitive Biases and Social Engineering techniques to win the all important "Management Buy-in." How to overcome the shortcoming of techno-speak and embrace business speak.

Think of yourself as an Anthropologist, venturing into and exploring a strange, unusual culture, foreign to your own culture of Geekdom. You are the stranger unaccustomed to their ways, speech, and mannerisms. You are like Margaret Mead among the Samoan people. We have a relative who was in the Philippines with the Peace Corps sitting around the dinner table in a remote village when they passed her the platter of goat eyeballs. What do you do?

The success of your mission depends on your actions or more importantly your attitude!

Cognitive Biases (An Overview)

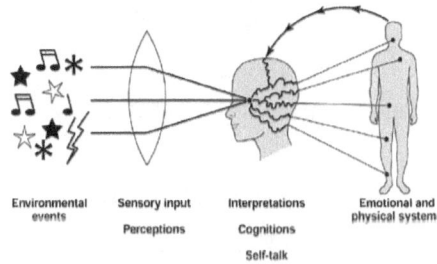

Environmental events · Sensory input · Perceptions · Interpretations · Cognitions · Self-talk · Emotional and physical systems

The following was extracted from the book Common Cognitive Biases: Examples and Challenges by the authors and available from Amazon. We have presented our finding of the effects of cognitive biases on security at several conferences, symposiums, and workshops. If you are interested in this or other books published by the authors, turn to the page at the end of the book for a link to Amazon.com listing this book and others by the authors.

Cognitive bias describes the inherent thinking errors that Homo sapiens make in processing information. Several have been verified empirically in the fields of cognitive science (psychology, anthropology, education, neuroscience, computer science) and behavioral economics while many others still need more rigorous scientific investigation.

Cognitive biases are thinking errors that prevent one from accurately understanding or interpreting reality, even when confronted with all the required data and evidence to form an accurate view of the situation. Many conflicts and mistakes are due to cognitive biases preventing people from coming to the same conclusions with the same evidence. Cognitive bias is intrinsic to human thought, and any systematic process of acquiring knowledge must include ways to control these biases.

Our thoughts, beliefs, and ideas about the world around us, both concrete and abstract, cause our brains to create a filter for us to receive information from our surroundings. Cognitive bias occurs when we have distortions in how we perceive and interpret facts, causing us to lack good judgment and make poor decisions. Like so many human traits these biases are influenced by human evolution and natural selection.

Numerous cognitive biases evolution, adaptive,

and became beneficial because they lead to more effective action in given contexts or enable faster decisions when faster decisions are of greater value for reproductive success and survival.

In our modern society, most cognitive biases are a result of a lack of appropriate mental mechanisms. This is a general fault in the human brain structure. This misapplication of a tool that was adaptive and beneficial under different circumstances a 100,000 to 1 millions years ago to simply our noisy mental processes.

The hidden ghosts of our brain are best adapted to help us with simple, concrete day-to-day problems. These cognitive biases interfere, given us false reading, causes us to make costly mistakes in highly mathematical or abstract problem solving such as differential equations, imaginary numbers international relationship, intra-company, and interpersonal interactions our modern life.

The notion of cognitive biases was introduced by Amos Tversky and Daniel Kahneman in 1972 and grew out of their experience of people's innumeracy, or inability to reason intuitively. Tversky, Kahneman, and colleagues demonstrated several replicable ways in which human judgments and decisions differ from rational choice theory, the basis of traditional economics . Tversky and Kahneman explained human differences in judgment and decision making in terms of heuristics. "Heuristics involve mental shortcuts which provide swift estimates about the possibility of uncertain occurrences (Baumeister & Bushman, 2010, p. 141). Heuristics are simple for the brain to compute but sometimes introduce "severe and systematic errors" (Tversky & Kahneman).

A cognitive bias refers to a systematic pattern of deviation from norm or rationality in judgment. Individuals create their own "subjective social reality" from their perception of the input. An individual's construction of social reality, not as behaviorist psychology would state, the external input, dictates their behavior in the social world. Thus, cognitive biases may sometimes lead to perceptual distortion, inaccurate judgment, illogical interpretation, or what is broadly called irrationality. Cognitive biases enable faster decisions when timeliness is more valuable than accuracy. These "hidden ghosts" are a "by-product" of the human brain's processing limitations resulting from a lack of appropriate mental mechanisms, bounded rationality , or simply from a limited capacity for information processing. (Servitor)

The authors have noted a continually evolving and growing list of cognitive biases that have been identified over the last six decades of research on human judgment and decision-making in cognitive science, social psychology, and behavioral economics in our text <u>Common Cognitive Biases: Examples and Challenges</u>. Kahneman and Tversky (1996) argue that cognitive biases have efficient, practical implications for areas including clinical judgment, entrepreneurship, finance, and management. The authors of this text are presenting a subset of cognitive biases, emphasizing how cognitive biases affect marketing, sales, and the process that leads to decision making by solving conflict resolution and problem solving and providing a winning buy-in from management.

Despite several decades of research and experimentation, no comprehensive theory of what creates or causes cognitive biases has emerged. Grouping and/or categorizing cognitive biases are not straightforward so making listings of cognitive basis are a grab bag at best, which has no quantitative cognitive science research, or experimentation to support the grouping. (Dougherty) A 2012 Psychological Bulletin article suggested that at least eight seemingly unrelated biases can be produced by the same informational and generative theoretic mechanism that assumes noisy information processing during storage and retrieval of information in human memory. (Hilbert)

There are numerous reasons, theories, and debates as to why Homo sapiens have a heuristic toolkit and cognitive biases with no single model having won the lead. The authors personally like the System 1, System 2 viewpoint. But the question remains as to why cognitive biases are cross-cultural, cross-racial, cross-social-economics-status in the human brain's processing.

The definition of each cognitive bias discussed below was pulled from the various articles used in the text and from a group of researchers at the Royal Society of Account Planning (RSAP). The RSAP defined cognitive biases In the Visual Study Guide to Cognitive Biases, as "psychological tendencies that cause the human brain to draw incorrect conclusions."

Such biases are thought to be a form of "cognitive shortcut," often based upon rules of thumb, and include errors in statistical judgment, social attribution, and memory. These biases are a common outcome of human thought, and often drastically skew the reliability of anecdotal and legal evidence. This phenomenon is studied in behavioral economics, cognitive science, and social psychology."

"We all have a multitude of cognitive biases influencing our decisions. "...cognitive biases lay below the surface of a prospect's consciousness they still play a role in their behavior during the sales process." (Renahan) Brudner states "they're built into the fabric of our thought -- so to us, they just seem normal." Marketers and Salespeople who are in the *field of persuasion have benefited from learning how to spot and use cognitive biases."* Knowing cognitive biases and how they affect human behavior are a boost to anyone involved in marketing, sales or social engineering.

Categories or
Grouping of Cognitive Biases

Belief and Decision-Making Biases

The deviation from what is generally expected

"These influence us when we are about to make a major decision, whether it is to buy something, claim something in a discussion, to choose where or how to stand in a debate and etc." (Servitor) Continuing our clarification of decision-making biases, many of these affect belief formation in business and economic decisions, as well as, human behavior in general. They arise as a replicated result to a particular condition when confronted with a given situation. Finally, "Cognitive biases steer our decision making in subtle-but-definite ways," as Benson stated. They might make us a little more Pollyanna-ish, somewhat more self-centered, a bit more negative, slightly more what-have-you-done-for-me-lately, or a little more something else. Little, but measurable, pushes to our decision in reactive directions." (Benson)

Social (Attribution) Biases

People involved in an action,
the actor, view thing differently
from people not involved, the observers.

"These influence us when it come to understanding ourselves, our actions in relation to other people and their actions." (Servitor) An attribution bias affects the way we determine who or what was responsible for an event or action (attribution). It is a cognitive set that may interfere with social interaction. Wikipedia continues by stating that "Attribution biases," social biases, "typically take the form of *actor/observer differences*: people involved in an action (*actors*) view things differently from people not participating (*observers*). These discrepancies are often caused by asymmetries in availability, known as salient. Taylor and Fiske (1975) concluded that "the more salient a potential causal agent is, the greater the causal role observers will assign to the agent in accounting for particular outcomes of events." (Jones) In the book Tradecraft Primer published by the CIA, Attribution biases (Social) are observed as "Behavior of others is attributed to some fixed nature of the person or county, while our own behavior is attributed to the situation in which we find ourselves" A "bias in perceiving causality." Other examples include "Why don't they just..." or "Armchair quarterback."

Memory biases

Either enhances or impairs
the recall of a memory
or alters the content of a reported memory

This category of biases influences how what, and why we remember certain things the way we do. (Servitor) Wikipedia defines memory bias as a cognitive bias that enhances or impairs the recall of memory

    1. the chances that the memory will be remembered at all.

    2. the amount of time it takes for it to be remembered.

    3. a combination of both

    4. There is an alteration of the content of a reported memory.

As with all Cognitive Biases, there are many types of memory bias; "...cues such as the ease with which a scenario or event comes to mind, and the frequency of such events in memory may significantly influence our estimation of their actual likelihood". (Jones) "We've established that your memory of the past is unreliable and your perception of the present is highly selective." (Aamodt and Wang)

What follows is a brief definition and example of the Cognitive Biases used in this text.

> *"Last time it wasn't so bad."*
> *In fact, it was actually worse!*
> *"I'm 99% sure, which means*
> *I'm wrong 40% of the time."*

Cognitive Biases discussed as alluded to in this text

What follows is a description of the Cognitive Biases that apply to marketing, sales, and decision making discussed, or alluded to, in this text. Each paragraph contains the name of the cognitive bias, a discussion, an example or two, and which topic it is applied.

For a more detailed study about Cognitive Biases and Cognitive Science check out the following books under the References section. Predictably Irrational, Revised and Expanded Edition: The Hidden Forces That Shape Our Decisions by Dan Ariely

Thinking, Fast and Slow by Daniel Kahneman The 25 Cognitive Biases: Uncovering The Myth

Of Rational Thinking by Charles Holm

Influence: The Psychology of Persuasion by Robert Cialdini

50 Cognitive Biases For An Unfair Advantage in Entrepreneurship by Adrian Nantchev

Ambiguity Effect: The authors believe that this bias is one of the cornerstones of Behavioral Economics. From Wikipedia; The ambiguity effect is a cognitive bias where decision making is affected by a lack of information, or "ambiguity." The effect implies that people tend to select options for which the probability of a favorable outcome is known, over an option for which the likelihood of a favorable outcome is unknown.

Category: Belief and Decision Bias

Example:
- ☐ Salespeople often show a costly item first, making all other options seem more affordable.
- ☐ Most people would choose a regular paycheck over the unknown payoff of a business venture.

- ☐ If a board of directors is deciding whether to keep with the same strategy that is continuing to lose steam or take a chance on a new one—they're likely to feel an urge to stick to what they've seen and understand.

- ☐ "The devil you know." Think about ordering a familiar dish at a new restaurant versus ordering something that sounds great but is new to your palate.

Applied to: Marketing and Sales

Related to: Loss Aversion

Anchoring Bias: A tendency to rely on or make a decision based on a past reference or a single trait, or a single piece of information, or the first option presented to you. "Whether for good or for bad, the first piece of information we receive about a person or situation will color our overall perception." (Brudner) All further information about an individual or situation is judged by the initial details of the meeting; called the anchor.

Category: Belief and Decision Bias

Example:

- ☐ All the stuff about how first impressions matter is real. How you introduce yourself and your product, your security product, policy, or procedures does in fact matter.
- ☐ The first snippet of information that you present to senior management should set a positive tone, a win/win for the listener. Show what you want up front. Don't build up to it as we do in a scientific manner. Present what is your desired outcome first then add supporting material as need.
- ☐ Presenting the specific information at the top of the discussion ensures that you and management are thinking toward the same goal from the start.

Applied to: Sales, Decision Making

Also, know as Focalism

Availability effect: is a mental shortcut that relies on immediate examples that come to a given person's mind when evaluating a particular topic, concept, method or decision.

Category: Belief and Decision Bias

Example:

- ☐ You have been watching the latest news reports about the number of car thefts around the country. Because you lack the time or resources, you make a judgment that this is happening in your community. You make a decision that car thefts are more common than they really are in your area. Faced with the need for an immediate decision, the availability heuristic allows people to make a quick decision, Many time these conclusions are incorrect.
- ☐ Like other biases, the availability bias can be useful at times. But it tends to lead to problems and errors in judgment. Examples of reports such as child abductions, airplane accidents, and train derailments have a tendency to lead people to the belief that such events are the norm.
- ☐ After hearing reports about people losing their jobs, you start ruminating that you're in trouble of losing your position. You start lying awake in bed each night worrying that you are about to be fired.
- ☐ After watching "Shark Week," you begin to think that incidences of attacks are a common occurrence. Now, you have a

trip to the beach, and you refuse to go swimming in the ocean because of the high number of attack.

Applied to: Sales

Related to or also known as illusory truth effect, or reality effect or the illusion-of-truth effect

Bandwagon Effect: The tendency to do (or believe) things because many other people do (or believe) the same.

Category: Belief and Decision Bias

Example:
- ☐ Any type of Fads.
- ☐ Voting for the person who appears to be winning even if you don't like them

Applied to: Marketing, Sales

Related to: Groupthink, Herd Behavior

Confirmation Bias: The tendency to search for or interpret information in a way that confirms one's preconceptions. In conversations the impulse to lock onto a part of a talk that confirms your existing beliefs, values, and perceptions.

Category: Belief and Decision Bias

Example:
- ☐ Scientific beliefs (vaccinations, climate changes, etc.)
- ☐ political parties
- ☐ sport fans
- ☐ Imagine that you're researching a potential product. You think that the market is growing , you find information that supports this belief. Because of your research. you decide that the product will sell quite well, with backers and an extensive marketing campaign you launch your product...to a total failure. Everything is wrong; market did not grow, fewer customers are generated, the product tanks. It is an example of interpreting the productivity growth in a way that reinforces your preconceptions.

Applied to: Marketing, Sales, Decision Making

Curse of Knowledge: When better-informed people find it extremely difficult to think about problems from the perspective of lesser-informed people. "The curse of knowledge is a cognitive bias that occurs when, in predicting others' forecasts or behaviors, individuals are unable to ignore the knowledge they have that others do not have, or when they fail to disregard information already processed. Things become second nature, so we forget about details, leaving others in the dark.

Category: Belief and Decision Bias

Example:
- ☐ People in technical fields or specialties filed
- ☐ Where to begin when teaching a language?
    - ☐ An example of the curse of knowledge is demonstrated in a classroom setting, where teachers, or subject experts, have difficulty teaching novices because they cannot put themselves in the position of the student. A brilliant professor may no longer remember the problems that a young student may be encountering when learning a new subject.

☐ Telling someone how to build a watch when they just ask for the time.

Applied to: Marketing, Sales, Decision Making

Decoy Effect: The Decoy Effect comes into play when consumers are choosing between two choices and have a preference, but change their preference when a third strategically priced choice is offered.

Category: Belief and Decision Bias

Example:

☐ When you have two options, users will typically pick the cheaper options; this is not the option you as the salesperson wanted. How do you encourage the buying of the more expenses option and have the buyer believe it is their idea? This is a perfect situation for the decoy effect! Now, you add a third option the decoy; it is priced close to the more expensive option. By doing this, the higher cost option appears to be the better buy. Buyers will feel that they are getting the better deal and purchase the more expensive option, which is what you wanted in the first place. So, when presented with two options buyers tend to buy the cheaper option, but when a third strategically option is placed closer to the higher price option, the buyer will purchase the more expensive option.

☐ Online pricing offers an excellent example of the decoy effect. Here is a case from a leading magazine. Here is the setup from the magazine with three options for their potential subscribers. Option 1. a digital subscription ($50), Option 2. a print subscription ($125), Option 3. Both a print + digital subscription ($125). They are focusing you on the third option they wanted to in the beginning.

☐ You can use an optical illusion with the decoy effect; it involves where you place of the decoy. Because most buyers will pick the middle option, you have to set the bait closer to the more expensive option it appears to be just a small increase in money for a much bigger return.

☐ Now could you use the middle position equally separated from one another options? The answer is by placing the more expensive and preferred option in the middle position.

Applied to: Marketing and Sales

Related to: Asymmetric Dominance effect

Framing: Using an approach or description of the situation or issue that is too narrow. In addition, drawing different conclusions based on how data is presented.

Category: Belief and Decision Bias

Example:
- ☐ Positive vs. negative framing only 3 people failed vs. at least 258 failed!
- ☐ Participants saw a film of a traffic accident and then answered questions about the event, including the question 'About how fast were the cars going when they contacted each other?' Other participants received the same information, except that the verb 'contacted' was replaced by either *hit, bumped, collided,* or *smashed.* Even though all of the participants saw the same film, the wording of the questions affected their answers. The speed estimates (in miles per hour) were 31, 34, 38, 39, and 41, respectively.
  - ☐ One week later, the participants were asked whether they had seen broken glass at the accident site. Although the correct answer was 'no,' 32% of the participants

who were given the 'smashed' condition said that they had. Hence the wording of the question can influence their memory of the incident.

☐ A keystone of sales and social engineering.

    ☐ Changing the frame changes the context, which changes our interpretation, and consequently our experience.

    ☐ The more knowable and trained a person is in a specified field the more likely there are to make irrational, including life and death, decisions than an individual who is new or less indoctrinated to the specified area. That individual who is ingrained in their field will base their decisions on the superficial wording of the information rather than the real facts and probabilities. Someone who has not been trained in cross-cultural and/or cross-discipline fields will analyze the facts not the "word-tree" of the speaker.

Applied to: Sales, Decision Making

Related to:

Fundamental Attribution: The tendency for people to over-emphasize personality-based explanations for behaviors observed while under-emphasizing the role and power of situational influences on the same behavior. Walk a mile in the other person's shoes. Which means to truly understand a person's reasoning, behavior, or reaction you must see the situation from their point of view. When we judge others' actions, we tend to give too much weight to their character and not enough to the circumstances in which they acted. While no accepted explanation is shared by everyone for this cognitive bias, numerous hypotheses have been offered up for the cause of this error in human thinking. Interesting, this is one of the few cognitive thinking error that does have cultural differences that affect the explanation of this error. The research conducted has shown that groups from an "individualistic" culture are more inclined to exhibit the Fundamental Attribution, which groups from a collectivistic culture are not as likely to show this error in thinking.

Category: Social/Attributional Bias

Example:
- ☐ A classic example is a person who goes for their driving test. They fail and blame the situation, the car, the tester, the road conditions, etc. but not themselves, their lack of studying, their lack of preparation. Now, if they had passed, then it would have been that they are great, wonderful.
- ☐ If Alice saw Bob trip over a rock and fall, Alice might consider Bob to be clumsy or careless (personal/dispositional). But if Alice tripped over the same rock herself, she would be more likely to blame the placement of the rock (situational).

Applied to: Decision Making

See also: Actor-Observer bias, Group Attribution Error or Attribution Effect, Positivity Effect, Negativity Effect, or Correspondence bias.

Gambler's Fallacy: The tendency to think that future probabilities are altered by past events when in reality they remain unchanged. The belief that events are in a fixed ratio of occurrence. The Journal of Risk and Uncertainty defined, in1994, the gambler's fallacy as "the belief that the probability of an event is decreased when the event has occurred recently."

Category: Belief and Decision Bias

Example:

☐ Flipping a coin is always 50/50 that it will be heads or tails but believing that one surface will be greater than the other based on past performance.

☐ Lady Luck is smiling on me tonight.

☐ In playing the roulette table the last four spins of the wheel had the ball land on the color black, you may want to believe that the next turn will land the ball on a red color. Just the opposite, you may think the ball will continue to fall on the color black.

☐ During the middle age, people would gamble that the birth of a child would be a boy or girl. They had no idea about how the sex of a child was determined.

Applied to: Sales, DecisionMaking

See also: Monte Carlo fallacy, the negative recency effect, or the fallacy of the maturity of chances

Hyperbolic Discounting: is the tendency for people to have a stronger preference for more immediate payoffs relative to later payoffs. Hyperbolic discounting leads to choices that are inconsistent over time – people make choices today that their future selves would prefer not to have done, despite using the same reasoning. This is hyperbolic discounting in action.

Category: Belief and Decision Bias

Example:
- ☐ NOW is always better than later.
- ☐ There was a famous research experimental psychology study (Stanford) in delayed gratification where the researcher "Offer a toddler a piece of candy now or two pieces of candy 15 minutes later.
- ☐ It was shown in adults that hyperbolic discounting doesn't really change much as we grow up.

Applied to: Sales

Related to: Current Moment Bias, Present-Bias, Dynamic Inconsistency.

IKEA effect: The tendency for people to place a disproportionately high value on objects that they partially assembled themselves, such as furniture from IKEA, regardless of the quality of the end result.

Category: Belief and Decision Bias

Example:
- ☐ Involving everyone in the company in making a decision will share the ownership of the project.
- ☐ Every time you see the pride of the worker, who says something like, " I helped make that," you see the IKEA effect.

Applied to: Marketing, Sales, Decision Making

Illusory Truth Effect: A self-reinforcing process in which a collective belief gains more and more plausibility through its increasing repetition in public discussions or reports.

Category: Belief and Decision Bias

Example:
- ☐ Keep repeating something long enough, and it will become real.
- ☐ Political slogans and campaign rhetoric.
- ☐ Advertising slogans and jingles are used as popular and catchy ways to make us pay attention and repeat the advertiser's message to ourselves. (See Rhyme-As-Reason.)

Applied to: Sales

Related to: Also known as the **truth effect** or the **illusion-of-truth effect**

Loss Aversion Bias: Loss aversion is the human tendency to try to avoid loss over acquiring a gain. To put it in a more colloquial term, it is worse to lose one's jacket than to find one. It has been suggested that psychologically, losses are twice as powerful. Once burned, twice shy. Neuroscience points out that humans may be hardwired to be loss averse due to our psychobiological evolution and its pressure on gains and losses.

Category: Belief and Decision Bias

Example:
- ☐ In the early days of humanoids, the loss of a day's food could amount to death. It appears that "serial gamblers" are the exception to loss aversion.

Applied to: Sales

See also: Sunk cost, Endowment effect

Ostrich effect: Ignoring an obvious negative situation.

Category: Belief and Decision Bias

Example:
- ☐ That check engine light that is glowing can't be ignored for long.
- ☐ Those attacks on the network can't be ignored.
- ☐ Insider threats must be taken seriously.

Applied to: Sales, Decision Making

Related to: Loss Aversion, Elephant in the Room

Overconfidence Bias: Excessive confidence in one's own answers to questions or ability to solve a problem. This is a well-established and much studied cognitive bias. Individuals will identify subjective confidence in their judgments is greater than the objective accuracy in reality. The best example is that people who rate their answer as 99% sure are incorrect 40% of the time. In the literature overconfidence can be divided into three distinct ways as stated in Wikipedia:

1. An overestimation of one's actual performance;
2. An overplacement of one's performance relative to others;
3. An overprecision in expressing unwarranted certainty in the accuracy of one's beliefs

The Overconfidence Bias can be shown in many different major areas.

1. Overestimation
2. Over-precision
3. Over-placement

Overconfidence is called the most "pervasive and potentially catastrophic" of all the cognitive biases. It has been the source of countless lawsuits, strikes, wars, and stock market bubbles and crashes, to list just a few.

Category: Belief and Decision Bias

Example:
- ☐ In playing trivia, my teammates will ask are you sure? And I say yes, I'm 99% sure but I'm wrong 40% of the time.
- ☐ In many instances you will hear people state "tell me the best choice," I don't have the time to weed out all the options. To help with this thinking have two options to explore before making a decision.
- ☐ Use a decision team. Multiple people are exploring the options from various angles and possibilities.
- ☐ Use a systematic approach to studying and making decisions, not you "gut feeling." Use this framework is making decisions and modify the structure to refine your and your's team approach.
- ☐ There is nothing wrong with bringing in "outsiders" to help analyze a decision or review your decision framework.

Applied to: Decision Making

Related to: Dunn-Kruger effort

Rhyme-as-Reason: is a cognitive bias whereupon a saying or aphorism is judged as more accurate or truthful when it is rewritten to rhyme. If you want to leave a lasting impression about your representation, you should develop a rhyme of the key points.

Category: Belief and Decision Bias

Example:
- ☐ "If the gloves don't fit, then you must acquit."
- ☐ "Loose lips sink ships."
- ☐ "Red sky at morning, sailors take warning."
- ☐ "birds of the feather, flock together."
- ☐ "Leaves of three, let it be."

Applied to: Marketing and Sales

Related to: Eaton-Rosen phenomenon, Illusory Truth Effect

Prospect Theory: Human love the status quo, we want certainty in our life, day-after-day the same thing within a narrowly defined range. We will sacrifice income opportunities for certainty. For close to 400 hundred years classical economist believed and developed theories, algorithms based on the idea that human made rational decisions. In the early to mid- seventy a group of cognitive scientist espoused the idea that humanity are irrational beings who are influenced by our environment and the interpretation of our environment much more than we would like to believe. Because of this, we make decisions that are not in our best interest. Behavioral economics breaks down the human decision-making process. Using Prospect theory, we begin to understand the factors that affect decision making and the choices we make.

Several ideas that Prospect theory and Behavioral economics bring that helps in understanding cognitive biases and how to apply cognitive biases to marketing, sales, and social engineering includes:
- ☐ "Incentives are the cornerstone of modern life."

- ☐ "Knowing what to measure, and how to measure it, can make a complicated world less so."
- ☐ "Conventional wisdom is often wrong."
- ☐ "Correlation does not equal causality."

From Steven Levitt and Stephen Dubner.

Category: Not a bias, but a cornerstone of Behavioral Economics and related to several biases.

Example:
- ☐ Staying with the status quo when it would be best to go with something new
- ☐ Taking out loans that we cannot afford
- ☐ Smoking though we know it is harmful
- ☐ Purchasing items things we do not need
- ☐ Saving too little for a "raining day" or retirement.

Applied to: Marketing, Sales

Related to: Ambiguity, Loss Aversion, and several others.

Peak-End Rule: We are willing to sacrifice our comfort as long as there is a positive outcome in sight. We will remember the apex and the end. Memories of the whole will be determined by the feeling you had at the moment your brain considered to be the crest and the time of the ending. It's not that your brain forgets the information, it that the brain filter out and conscience on the peak and the end of an event.

Category: Belief and Decision Bias
- ☐ Taking out loans that we cannot afford

Example:
- ☐ Music is a great example of the Peak-End Rule. While writing this book, we had Beethoven's Saints' Day Overture playing. It's easy to see and feel the climactic point that invites the listener to become involved in the music, then it ends on a beautiful positive chord, making one want to say, out loud, where can I find more of that music?
- ☐ Another example is the old-time preacher who knew how to build the sermon to a fever pitch that everyone could remember, then softly and positively bring the closing with the inspirational message that you could be one of the chosen, ending with a great

invitational song, with words like "come home, come home...."

Applied to: Sales

Projection Bias: is a feature in human thinking where one thinks that others have the same priority, attitude or belief that one harbors oneself, even if this is unlikely to be the case. In the article written by Dvorsky, he discusses that "we tend to assume that most people think just like us - though there may be no justification for it." We have a tendency to overestimate how typical and average we are, and assume that a consensus exists on matters when there is no real consensus. This bias appears in the group that believes more people on the outside of the group agree or are like them than is the case.

Category: Social/Attributional Bias

Example:
- ☐ I knew a brother and sister who were from the US but grew up in India. All the fathers were engineers of some type. All the mothers were also college graduates. The group living in this compound were

from many different countries. From this small group, the image is that everyone from the US goes to college. I show this brother and sister the real statistics for college bound individuals in the US; they were shocked how reality was different from the projection they grew-up with in India.

Applied to: Decision Making, Sales

Status Quo Bias: The tendency for people to like things to stay relatively the same. Know as the "Steady State" in economics.

Category: Belief and Decision Bias

Example:
- ☐ Comfort zone think of HGTV International House Hunters. Watch the TV show where people move oversea to another country, and they want the new house or apartment to be just like the one they left in their countries of origin.
- ☐ Want an individual to use your brand of browser or email, then have it automatically install on the system and be the default for that system. Most people will just use what's is installed.

People will defend the default option, not at would already there, but it the best, because it was the default.
□ Always give people a default option plan when offering choices. Individuals are naturally predisposed to select the default. Frame your presentation with a default option.

Applied to: Sales, Marketing, Decision Making

Related to: loss aversion, endowment effect, and system justification biases

In Conclusion

Cognitive Biases happen in day-to-day life; there impact is exponentially worse in the business world because they can affect so many people. There are numerous reasons, theories, and debates as to why Homo sapiens have a heuristic toolkit and cognitive biases. No one model has won the lead. The authors personally like the System 1, System 2 viewpoint. Besides the questions of why Homo sapiens have cognitive biases and which models best explain our heuristic toolkit, it remains a mystery as to why cognitive biases are cross-cultural, cross-racial, cross-social-economics status in the way they affect humans.

The human brain is conducting "billions and billions" of processes and calculations all the time. The combination of our mental processes and the environment causes the brain to search for general "rules of thumb" to apply to various circumstances. This worked wonderfully millions of years ago but not so well in modern society as cognitive biases continue to trip up our decision-making process.

We will all be blameworthy of falling victim to various cognitive biases unless we keep up our guard . The authors would recommend using the "Scientific Method" to challenge Cognitive Biases.

We will end with some common traits in faulty decision making caused by Cognitive Biases.

<u>Knee-jerk reaction</u>: Making a fast and intuitive decision when a slow and deliberate decision is needed.

<u>Occam Razor</u>: Assume the most obvious decision is the best decision.

<u>Silo Effect</u>: Use too narrow an approach in making a decision.

<u>Conformational effect</u>: Focus on information that affirms your beliefs and assumptions.

Marketing

Introduction:
Most think of marketing as selling consumable goods like soup, tires, or pizza. Security is a product. it is our product and we, as a security professional, we do a terrible job of marketing that product to our customers, the very people who need our product, services, policies, procedures the most. "When people think about marketing, they think about external marketing" (McLellan).

McLellan continues "..no business can afford to forget to actively and regularly market to its own employees. I'm not sure why business owners and leaders don't see the importance of marketing to their employee base, but it's often either completely forgotten or it's one of the smallest line items in the budget."

In terms of marketing security, we must remember, "Typically, the employees who are paid the least and told the least - interact with your customers the most." (McLellan). As security professionals, we must understand that companies are pyramid shaped and we need to know who is going to interact the most with security issues.

What do you do?:

Where does the security staff spend the majority of their day? Usually the office, laboratories, unclassified or classified labs. In other words, does your security staff spent their time huddled around a computer, researching and correcting problems? Does your security staff spend their time with people outside of security, with business types? In all likelihood, that valuable time is spent at the computer and with fellow security geeks. Security professionals need to get out of the labs and interact with other employees of the company. It's important to have lunch with them, explain the what, where, when, and how of security, share your exasperation of new strict, bizarre, and pain in the backside rules mandated and dictated to the security team by outside forces. Most users think that security policies, procedures, rules, etc. are the dream child of the company security department. They don't know where the rules originated or why they even exist.

Apha, Uno Numero, ml' wa'

Most people, and senior management, in particular, have no idea what security does for the company except get in the way of the business making a profit. "Get to know the members of your executive team, understand what motivates them and how they are judged by their boss." (Birmingham) You may very well be the alpha dog, uno numero, or in Klingon, the ml' wa' of geeks in your security-techno world but that doesn't mean you will be successful in the world of business. Avoid the techno babble and adapt business speak to communicate positivity with senior managers. It is imperative to learn the language their speak.

Stating Requirements are not Enough:
It's not enough to say it's a requirement! This is our most common mistake in security; we start quoting rules, regulations, and laws. This standard approach has been used in all walks of life. "If you don't do ... you will be punished," we must try a different approach one of encouragement, or training, or positive reinforcement. Like Dr. Alan Smith of Jacksonville State University said long along,"What if the police stopped you and gave you a reward for driving correctly?" Today we could use traffic cameras to send safe, smart, law-abiding drivers a gift card. Behaviorism psychology at its best. We need to develop somehow marketing strategies that cause

people in our company to emulate the old marketing campaign of the railroad and government:

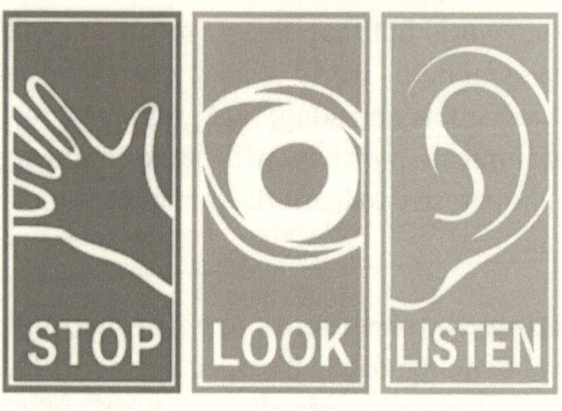

Many companies have an annual Security Awareness campaign. The entire company is flooded with security awareness posters, mandatory briefing, and emails (and emails, and emails!) about the punishment of not following security policy. This is one of our biggest problems, as an article from Amsterdam Printing stated, "...don't recommend bombarding your employees with all of the ideas at once." Many things are beyond Security's control, like employees'

happiness with the company or physical comfort of the working environment. But you can get them to be a security team member. There may be an employee hoarding "red staplers, " but your data is safe because the employee feels like a part of the security team.

We will continue with the Amsterdam Printing discussion of the five things to do to get employees to promote your business. We will modify their discussion because we are concentrating on one group within the company (in case you forgot!), security.

Amsterdam Printing discusses the idea of "listening to your employees." Employees want to grumble and complain about new policies, procedures, and requirements. Any change in their daily routine will produce one of the most common complaints heard. "This new rule is interfering with me getting my work done," or "I'm not going to meet my customer's deadline. " Most people will feel better if you listen to them, show understanding, demonstrate that you care for their circumstances.

I once lead a group of talented software engineers. We developed a one of a kind application that every month we would get new requirements and then deliver these requirements to the customer at the Pentagon by the end of the month. After presenting our new requests from our customer, I would let the team complain and grumble and tell me how it couldn't be done. After about thirty minutes I would stop everyone and ask one question. "Now that you told me how it couldn't be done, now tell how it could be done." The brainstorming began, with no idea too strange or bizarre. We worked our way inward to a viable solution, and everyone was happy, well as happy as could be. People may not be happy with new security requirements but they will respond positively to new ideas when you listen, and then they will find ways to live with it. By taking steps like this, Security has created an "open and welcoming culture" where employees feel invited to give feedback. This will increase positive participation by everyone.

Like all the articles reviewed, Amsterdam Printing states that security must provide regular training and resources. Most companies say that they do once a year mandatory training. We have to move to new solutions so that training is regularly presented, not the yearly face-to-face lecture. We also need to learn to use social media to broadcast security education. We have to move from the 1990s idea of posters on the wall and a yearly lecture on the evils of lax security to a more interactive daily marketing strategy. Social media is a perfect place for this interactive security training. Blogs, posts, games, electronic posters, etc. would help to engage the new workforce of employees.

Strategies are needed for distributing, nurturing, and tracking to ensure our customers and users are an essential part of security. All too often, employee input is overlooked when it comes to processes and procedures. By seeking out their recommendations and showing trust in their judgment, they will feel empowered and encouraged to promote the product - and our product is security! In too many companies, "employees are typically an untapped resource when it comes to content creation and distribution. Involving them in your content marketing will not only help improve and expand the reach and impact of your content, but it will also increase engagement internally, giving employees a feeling of brand ownership and pride. " (Fradin) And again our brand is security!

Putting it to use:

Nelson explained in his article that "the goal of Marketing is to educate the customer, employee." Our users must be trained about the importance of security, not browbeaten into submission.

The second goal is to make your targeted group feel a part of the team, the company, and the security campaign.

The third goal is to engage our customers to provide feedback We may not always like what they have to say, but they need the outlet.

After nurturing a ground swell of support for security objectives you can then move on to the fourth goal of marketing -- security benefits to senior management and their shareholders' bottom line.

In marketing, develop your own poster (or encourage employees too) for the company wall or social media space using the "Rhyme-As-Reason" (Brudner) effect to create earworms to help employees remember to practice good security habits. Seventy-five years after its creation, years before we were born, we still know "Loose Lips Sink Ships." We will continue our investigation about the Rhyme-As-Reason bias in the chapter on Sales.

Market the IKEA effect, so employees feel that they have a hand in creating, maintaining, and having a positive influence on the company security goals, techniques, and procedures for the enterprise.

Provide weekly emails to all employees about security best practices. Examples could include security alerts, fun stories about security, stupid security tricks:

Like the USB found in the parking lot and what people did. Another great story is from years ago where people were offered a pen, yes an ink pen, if people would share their password.

You just can't make this stuff up. People would enjoy reading these stories, talk about them around the "bubbler" and

Security needs to be known for developing a secure system to defend the missile defense system that defends the nation.

without knowing it, learn about security.

Sales

Introduction:

The key to sales is the same as the key to social engineering: "You just ask for it" Mitnick (2002).

Sovezak's article entitled "Smarten Up Your Prospecting Calls with Social Engineering" referred to social engineering as "the most underutilized tool available to salespeople-and the one that has the greatest possible payoff. All it requires is that you take the time to do it, develop a sense of curiosity, and cultivate some conversational question techniques."

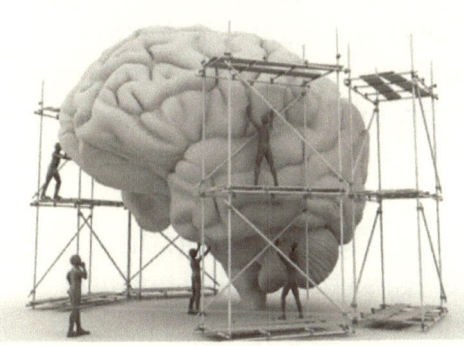

The human brain is a fascinating organ. It powerful processing ability is the envy of every computational cognitive neuroscientist. Self-driving cars, processing millions of calculations per seconds and using hundreds of sensors, still cannot match the human brain.

But, and this is a big but, our powerful processor of the human brain is still prone to make incredible, bizarre assumptions and totally illogical conclusions based on our caveman wiring that still believes that we need to guard against being eaten by lions, and tiger, and bears. Oh, my!

Because cognitive biases are a part of us, all of us, "They're built into the fabric of our thought - so to us, they just seem normal." (Brudner) Because of this, our customer (senior management) doesn't recognize the logic of our argument to purchase, install, and incorporate a particular security application, procedure, etc.

Brudner said in 2015, "Like it or not; these biases are part of us, so those in the business of persuasion can benefit from learning how to spot and play to them." So, are all salespeople social engineers? Based on the articles and research we've studied, we would have to answer in the affirmative.

Brudner's article, "How to use Psychological Biases to Sell Better and Faster" will be our foundation for discussing this chapter on sales.

We will now review and discuss the ten cognitive biases that, according to Brudner, relate to decision-making (sales). In each example, he helps you understand why you make the choices you do. He also goes a step further with a sales take away that will assist us in utilizing these quirks in our brain to sell better. In our case, winning management buy-in, using security for many of our case examples. A more detailed definition of each of the following Cognitive Biases can be found in the Chapter on, you guessed it, Cognitive Biases.

Ambiguity Effect in Sales

The Ambiguity Effect is a cornerstone of Behavioral Economics. Wikipedia defines it this way: "The ambiguity effect is a cognitive bias where decision making is affected by a lack of information, or "uncertainty." The effect implies that people tend to select options for which the probability of a favorable outcome is known, over an option for which the likelihood of a favorable outcome is unknown."

This bias causes our brain to react negatively to the unknown, commonly due to a lack of information - not data, but information. As Brudner states in his article, "Now, you can tell your significant other there's a scientific reason why it's so hard to venture away from your tried-and-true bar or restaurant."

My wife just walked in and said, "Let's go to the new restaurant I told you about." She has been to this establishment I have not. She is offering to buy the meal. We are going to ride past several places that I know have good food and/or service.

Which would you do? If your brain works like most people's, you'd probably opt for the known quality; you would not risk an unpleasant lunch by going to an unknown eatery.

We are strongly affected by the ambiguity effect, but when you combine the Loss Aversion bias to the equation, it can become an impossible barrier to overcome. Check out the Loss Aversion Bias in this chapter and see if you don't agree.

Putting it to use:
Your customers, employees, and your co-workers must be informed about the results

they should expect from implementing your security product, policy, or procedures. It is your responsibility to be able to answer their questions quickly or to fill in any gaps of knowledge they have that would prevent them from supporting you and making the right decision - the decision that you need.

Other ways to work with the ambiguity are to:

- ☐ Increase the customer comfort level.
- ☐ Compare known action results with the results of an unknown action.
    - ☐ Teaching a person to fish is better than giving them a fish
- ☐ Compare a known statistics to help with buy-in
    - ☐ Most risk of this type returns a 3.5 ROI; this risk has an ROI of 7.25
- ☐ Offer an assurance for them taking a risk. This shows that you believe.
    - ☐ Our boot camp = 60K job or your money back

Anchoring Effect in Sales

In Renahan's article "20 Weird Cognitive Biases Influencing Your Buyer's Decision," it's explained that "we all have a multitude of cognitive biases influencing our decision, regardless of who we're dealing with." Cognitive biases are always there, typically unknown to the individual but still influencing a prospect manager's consciousness. They can play a role in how others will change their behavior in the decision process, to support you or to reject your security product, policy, or procedures.

The Anchoring Bias is one of the most studied of the cognitive biases. Renahan explained that it is the tendency of people to be over-reliant on the first piece of information they hear, see, or are presented. The literature continues with the explanation that Anchoring is the tendency to rely on or make a decision based on a past reference or a single trait, or a single piece of information, or the first option presented to you.

"Whether for good or for bad, the first piece of information we receive about a person or situation will color our overall perception." (Brudner) All further information about an individual or situation is judged by the first details; this is called the anchor.

Putting it to use:

All that stuff about how first impressions matter is real. How you introduce yourself and your products, policies, or procedures does in fact matter. The first snippet of information that you present to senior management should set a positive tone and be a win/win for the listener. Submit what you want up front. Don't build up to it as we do in a scientific manner. Present what is your desire outcome first then add supporting material as needed.

Hyperbolic Discounting in Sales

In the late 1960s and early 1970s, psychologist Walter Mischel at Stanford University led a marshmallow experiment involving over 600 children. Each child was offered one marshmallow to eat immediately or two marshmallows if they waited 15 minutes or so. Only one-third of the children were able to hold off for that second marshmallow. This is hyperbolic discounting in action - NOW is better than later.

What does a group of young children have to do with us? Further research has shown that delayed gratification or hyperbolic discounting doesn't really change much as we grow up.

Hyperbolic discounting leads to choices that are inconsistent over time – people make choices today that their future selves would prefer not to have done, despite using the same reasoning. This is also known as current moment bias, present-bias, and related to Dynamic Inconsistency. (Wikipedia)

Think of Aesop's fables as you continue to read the following. Our brains are naturally biased toward rewards in the present vs. those in the future. "The "discounting" part of hyperbolic discounting refers to the fact that the perceived value of a reward decreases the farther it is in the future until the slope eventually flattens out." (Brudner)

Putting it to use:
Forget the grand "Great multi year" plan. Ask yourself and then prepare your presentation to meet the following;
- ☐ What can you do this budgetary quarter?
- ☐ What can you do the first quarter of the next fiscal year?

We must emphasize the quick and immediate results to senior management for a favorable decision to our proposal.

☐ You must be prepared to show how and when the benefit and/or rewards, the ROI, will start occurring, next month, next quarter, next fiscal year.

Follow-up with senior management on the positive results.

☐ Quickly demonstrate to management that they made the right decision.

☐ A quick demonstration will reinforce their belief that they can trust you and your decision making abilities in the future.

Bandwagon Effect in Sales

Most kids know that if they ask for something that all their friends are getting, parents are known for saying things like, "If all your friends jumped off a cliff, would you jump, too?" They are trying to prevent children from falling for the Bandwagon Effect. In essence, people have a tendency to believe or do things because other people believe or do them. This is also called Herd Behavior or Groupthink.

You may know that news sources don't start reporting the official poll results from the Eastern Time Zone until the Pacific Time Zone polls have closed for voting 3 hours later.

This is because of the Bandwagon Effect. In the past, it was noticed that if polls results showed a leader in the East, more people would vote for that candidate in the Pacific Time Zone than was expected. People were hopping on the bandwagon.

Just like the fads of Beanie Babies, Pet Rocks, and Troll Dolls, people naturally gravitate towards products or services they see other people using or political candidate who are receiving the most votes. The larger the number of supporters, buyers, users, etc., the more powerful the pull of this cognitive bias.

The bandwagon effect is seen in many facets of life, including what fashions are most stylish at the moment, which sports team is winning, and which stocks to buy. In the late 1990s, millions of dollars were invested in a number of tech startups that were mostly ideas on paper - the "dotcom bubble." Investors were clamoring to jump on the next big thing, and it created a feeding frenzy based on the trend of how everyone else was investing. This was a prime example of "jumping on the bandwagon." Most of the companies didn't last, and an enormous amount of money was lost.

Putting it to use:

The bandwagon bias is stronger than we think, so use it to your advantage. When trying to introduce new security products, policies, procedures, etc., play up the number of companies, or agencies that have already adopted the new security products with great success. If feasible obtain written testimonials. Even better, arm yourself with customers from another group, company, or agency that you can introduce to senior management.

If presenting as a team of two or more, you can create your own bandwagon effect by each person stating how great the new security product, policies, procedures, etc. is for the company.

Decoy Effect in Sales

The Decoy Effect is a great cognitive bias to use in sales. It sounds completely irrational but has been scientifically proven to work. You have actually seen it many times.

People have trouble choosing between two options. If a third option is provided, it can affect the decision based on which of the first two options it is similar to. Confused? Let's use an example. Which of the following would you purchase?

$7 $6.5 $3

Most diners will, of course, choose the $7 deal. The popcorn sales are using the 6.5 price to make the "special" price most attractive. If you list only the $3 and $7 dollar prices, most people will choose the $3 price because the larger $7 dollar is more than double the small price. But if you put a middle price choice that price is closer to the larger item people will buy the larger item. Notice the picture above, the price difference that the consumer will notice is only .50 cents more for the larger item. Selling the larger item is what you wanted all along.

Several universities have conducted the following experiment, with Duke University the most cited, to test this particular bias. Participants were given two dining choices: a five-star restaurant that was far away, and a three-star that was nearby. Most diners were torn between the two options. But after introducing the third possibility of a four-star restaurant even farther away than the five-star, the participants suddenly found that it was easy to choose the five-star option. The five-star restaurant was the best quality of the three and only slightly farther away in comparison with choice number three.

Putting it to use:

We have all learned the hard way that appearing in a meeting with way too many choices for senior management can be a total failure. It turns out that showing only two options can lead to a non-decision being made. If you know the top two options that you want senior management to pick.

1. Present your first choice first (Anchoring Effort).
2. Present your second choice.
3. Present a third option that is the most favorable one to help senior management make a decision. Like Brudner said in his article, "Use options to your advantage by presenting multiple versions of an offering or contract. If the prospect is really

struggling to decide, introduce a decoy that will reinforce their innate predisposition."

The decoy effect is a subtle and powerful tool. The effect is everywhere, influencing what and how we buy everything, from groceries to houses, where we eat, and what subscriptions we purchase. The decoy effect is almost too effective to believe.

Rhyme-As-Reason Effect in Sales

The idea of rhyming a slogan for marketing and sales has a long history. The military used "Loose Lips Sink Ships, " and Texaco told us to "Trust your car to the man who wears the star." Those examples are decades old, but they are still remembered today.

Matthew McGlone, Ph.D., a psychologist at Lafayette College in Pennsylvania speculates the "rhyme as reason" phenomenon may have had a hidden impact on the verdict in the murder trial of O.J. Simpson. When defense lawyer Johnnie Cochran intoned "If the glove don't fit, you must acquit!" Jurors, like everyone else, took notice and the quote became part of our pop culture.

Rhyming statements are perceived as more truthful (Gill).
- ☐ Do Your Part - Be Security Smart!
- ☐ When passwords are heard, losses are incurred.
- ☐ Loose clicks invite hacker tricks.
- ☐ Data spills provide no thrills (unless you're the bad guy).

And your parents thought that liberal art degree was a waste. It does pay to be a poet.

Putting it to use:

Develop your own
Rhyme-As_Reason effect
- ☐ Keep it positive
- ☐ Keep it short
- ☐ Anything but jargon
- ☐ Add a twist, surprise the reader
- ☐ Add wordplay

IKEA Effect in Sales

We love IKEA. We really like the furniture, and more importantly, we enjoy building the units together, wardrobes, dressers, headboards, etc., while listening to music, talking, laughing, and the bonding as a couple. This is what the IKEA effect is all about - the fact that people have a higher perceived value of items, projects, products when they have a meaningful input into its creation. The security element that the team had a hand in creating is view with more value and will defend better than the product of similar or possibly more superior. This applies to the selection of an "out of company" pre-build product if you get everyone involved in reviewing, selecting, discussing the product.

Putting it to use: Get senior management involved in selecting, customizing, let them put their own unique spin on to the security product, policy, or procedures. Like everyone else, the more senior management feels that it is really their idea (what you wanted them to choose), the more supportive they will be.

Polish Up Your Public Speaking Skills in Advance!

Illusion of Truth Bias in Sales

Repeating the same story is a powerful tool. The Illusion of Truth Bias has to be one of the most effective cognitive biases used by politicians, salespeople, and revolutionaries.

Keep stating your point until people believe it. Don't change your message, just keep repeating it. Dr. Jeremy Dean says "Repetition is one of the easiest and most widespread methods of persuasion."

This is one of those cognitive biases that just sounds too simplistic to be believable - that in real-life a persuasive message will increase its effect just by being repeated. The neuroscience of our brain causes a trigger based on "if it is familiar, it is also true." Researchers had studied individuals who would rate a statement as "more accurate" even when the statement was in fact "not true" if the speaker just repeated the statement.

As a technical scientific individual, "Geeks," we have to simplify our message or the reverse of the illusion of truth effect will come into play. If something is hard to think about, like calculus, economics, global problems; something that is hard to wrap our heads around it, then people tend not to believe it.

Putting it to use:
What is your message? Because of the nature of security, our message tends to be complex,

complicated, and hard to understand; we must simplify and repeat over and over, again and again, subtle variations of our message. The bottom line is to keep your message simple, easy to remember and easy to understand.

"If it's easy to understand, remember, and rhymes = TRUE."

Peak-End Rule in Sales

The Peak–End Rule is a tendency in which people judge an experience primarily based on how they felt at its peak and at its end. The literature defines the peak of the presentation as the most intense point. We do not base our positive or negative experience or impression on the sum total of the presentation. We don't forget the information before the peak or between the peak and the end of the presentation; we just don't use it to form our evaluation of the presentation.

Presentations should be handcrafted. It's not just presenting the information and walking away knowing that you give a sound "middle of the road" talk to the senior management where you spent an equal amount of discussion of the presentation, that you had a beginning, middle, and end all similar in time and energy. You must guide, direct, and energize the listener.

Music is a great example of the Peak-End Rule. While writing this book, we had Beethoven's Saints' Day Overture playing. It's easy to see and feel the climactic point that invites the listener to become involved the music, then it ends on a wonderful positive chord, making one want to say, out loud, where can I find more of that music?

Another example is the old-time preacher who knew how to build the sermon to a fever pitch that everyone could remember, then softly and positively bring the closing with the inspirational message that you could be one of the chosen, ending with a great invitational song, with words like "come home, come home...."

Putting it to use:
Do you hand-craft your presentation or are they as exciting as the drone of an aircraft engine? Do you practice your presentation, so you know when and where to drive the point home so the audience will remember? Does your presentation just kind of end or have you

built them, so there is a logical and positive conclusion?

> **Keys to the Peak-End Rule**
> ☐ Hit a deliberate high in your presentation.
> ☐ End-on a positive and interesting point.

> **The Three Bs**
> ☐ Be Brief
> ☐ Be Bright
> ☐ Be gone

Loss Aversion in Sales

We started this chapter discussing a cornerstone of behavioral economics, and so we will end with a list-discussion of fundamental cognitive biases, heuristic, effects with another foundation of behavior economics.

Loss aversion is the human tendency to try to avoid loss over acquiring a gain. To put it in a more colloquial term, it is worse to lose one's jacket than to find one. It has been suggested that psychologically, losses are twice as powerful. Once burned, twice shy.

Neuroscience points out that humans may be hardwired to be loss averse due to our psychobiological evolution and its pressure on gains and losses. In the early days of humanoids, the loss of a day's food could amount to death. It appears that "serial gamblers" are the exception to lose aversion, but that is a security paper for a later date.

"Losing something that is already owned has been shown to be far more painful than gaining something advantageous is pleasing." (Brudner) We can combine the knowledge about Loss Aversion bias and the framing bias to help sell our product. policies, procedures benefits to senior management

Putting it to use:
You can point out to senior management what they risk losing by staying with the status quo you demonstrate the inverse of loss aversion. By decreasing the risk of change you inversely prove the risk of staying with the status quo. Play down the loss, play up the profit.

In Conclusion

Emotions are a powerful motivator.

We have discussed the keys to successfully selling yourself and your ideas to senior managers. We have joined this to discussions in neuroscience research and shown how to practice and use our social engineering skills to achieve the object of providing better security for other customers. Maybe we can even congratulate the manager for his insight into the fact that he is not invincible to dragons.

"Most think that the core of sales is understanding the product, but in truth, it is about knowing the people to whom we are trying to sell the product" (Addison). Mr. Herrhusen, a former chairperson of Deutsche Bank, stated: "50 percent of business is psychology".

Addison continues by saying "Sales, as part of any business transaction, is all about people: our customer and how they think."

With all our talk of the neuroscience/psychology of sales here are five nut and bolts techniques to use in selling your managers on security. Again notice how this is geared toward business speak. The following is based on the "IT Business Edge" web site.

As professional security speaking to business types, we must learn their language. We must learn to present strategy, not "bolt-on" tactics. Sounds nice but what is the difference between a strategy and tactics, I'm a geek, this is that business speaks stuff. Roughly we can define a strategy as a how not a what. Tactics are the opposite the what not the how.

Like any other good business plan, a strategic long-term security roadmap is essential. Most upper-level management types don't understand bits and bytes, but they do understand risk and the financial impact on the business.

In meeting with senior management bring a prioritized set of risks to their attention, whether it be short-term or long-term.

Focus on the impact to the business, not how your new system or technology will work.

Give them a Timeline. Once you've presented the risk and severity of the security issue move to the solutions of the problem. Don't show up with only a list of problems, Show up with a list of solutions.

Show that you have a vision that will lead to successful implementation. Instead of using the Scientific approach with the emphasis on Problem - Solution – Timeline
Use the Business approach of
Solution – Problem - Timeline

In science we start with stating the problem, then the solution, then the timeline of implementing the solution. But in a business situation you may want to try starting with the solution, then the problem, finally ending with the timeline of the solution.

We as geeks must understand the reality that the implementation of the solution will normally have to occur selectively. Building a security process and procedure into your corporate culture will take time, learn to measure that process, learn how to share with everyone.

Don't over-mandate security requirements as the only reason to move forward. "Catch more flies with honey." People very quickly become numb to "everything is a crisis" As security professionals we must learn to triage the crisis.

Use data to your advantage if you can backup your numbers. Senior management live by numbers. Use data to show meaningful results to upper management on how the security policy, procedure, the application is improving the business bottom line. Try to remove guess work out of explaining why a new product, application, etc. is needed.

Finally, as we discussed in the opening of this chapter and as "IT Business Edge" presented on their website, we as security professional have to learn to network. You say you go to security meeting and are known across your local area. I understand, but I'm talking networking and building relationships with the various departments around the company. All the literature talks about how you will reap many benefits if only we will get out from behind our desk and socialize. "Raising your own profile in the organization through networking is another way to garner credibility regarding decisions and projects you propose."

Remember the game of sales is a game of social engineering. And social engineering is a game of the mind. You must understand how senior management thinks. You must understand their motivation to buy your security product, policy, or procedures. You must know how to move them to support your security solution. Remember you are the one that must change!

The following principles are taken from Robert Cialdini's <u>Influence: The Psychology of Persuasion.</u> **This** classic book on persuasion, explains the psychology of why people say "yes" even when they wanted to say "no." Dr. Cialdini goes a step further and explains how to apply these principles to marketing, sales, and decision making. I was first introduced to these ideas by my wife when we were dating. She has an extensive background in the art and science of sales.

To increase the potential of a deal use the principle of Reciprocity by preceding the request to buy with an unexpected gift. The most typical example of applying reciprocity is in marketing by giving "free samples" to potential customers. This principle is called "Reciprocity."

It is easier to keep a customer than to attract a new one because humans want to appear consistent by showing commitment. This principle is called "Consistency."

Humans follow trends; we are always observing what others are doing and then emulate that behavior. We want to be accepted, so we act the same as our society or culture. This is called "Social Proof," and is a powerful tool in marketing and sales. Keynes, the famous economist, stated, "It's easier to do wrong with the masses that to turn around and face the masses and tell the truth." This principle is called "Social Proof."

We are influenced by people we like; it can be as simple as physical appearance, dress in a way that aligned us together. We prefer individuals that speak the same language, Business language vs. techno-babble because we feel that they represent us. This principle is called "Likeability"

"People, in general, have a tendency to obey authority figures." Even if those authority figures are questionable, we will obey them. Want to increase sales? Have a confidence; authority person publicly supports your ideas, proposals, personality, etc. This principle is called "Authority."

Ever notice how an item is more attractive when its availability is limited. This is why limited time offer work or you can only buy so many of an items at one time. It is the imagine scarcity that causes people to want to purchase the product even more. As stated in this principle of "Scarcity," we buy more when we know we can not buy more.

Conflict Resolution =>
Problem Solving =>
Decision Making
The Curly Shuffle

Generally, authors talk about decision making pretending that everyone in the meeting, or sitting around the table are there for the common good, that they are all on the "same page," that everyone is respectful of each other; WRONG!

Before you can get to decision making you have to get everyone on the "same page." There may be interpersonal conflicts that must be resolved or cultural problems to be discussed before the decision-making process can move forward.

Another difference in the authors of this text approach is that we believe that it is you, the scientist, engineer, technology professional that must change. We have talked about changing your language, from geek to business. But you must also change your attitude about meeting and work with business individuals. You must change what your brain is telling you about the meeting, about the persons in the meeting, and about the behavior of the individuals.

There are several artifacts you must change to survive a business meeting with senior management. You must make your mind happy, by practicing "Mindfulness." Second, you must practice listening to understand, not listening to reply.

Throughout our text, we have used cognitive science, behavioral economics, and social engineering to illustrate strategies and tactics in marketing and sales to senior management. Again we will turn inward to our brain and learn to use skills from neuroscience, also referred to as brain science, to help us cope with those "creatures from another universe", also known as senior management, that are sitting across the table ripping your new security requirements, policies, procedures, products to shreds.

Yes, the situation is objectionable, painful, and disturbing. Yes, that senior manager is acting like a horse's patoot. Yes, this meeting is sinking faster than a lead balloon. Don't let the situation and behavior of another individual define and control you. Your left mind is going wild with interruptions, accusations, and incorrect interpretations of the situation you have lost focus and lost the meeting.

We must stop our rumination. We must learn "mindfulness," an ancient word for staying focus when all is crashing down around you. When you read about famous battles, or intense business negotiations, or government decision in a time of national crises you're reading about individuals who stay focused, who were mindful of the situation.

The meeting may still be lost, possibly a total disaster as far as your goals and objectives are concerned, but you are able to leave the meeting with a clear head, the present of mind about you to shake hand with each member of the senior management that have just ripped your beautiful, extraordinary ideas, project, etc. to shreds. You will be able to replay the meeting in your head, logically, to analyze where things got off track, how you could have done a better job during the presentation. Finally, you will be prepared to win the next battle for your Team.

Let us dive into this chapter by first discussing the two halves of the human brain, Left vs. Right. You must remember that the two halves of the brain are not always working together for our best interest.

According to Neuroscience, we can make ourselves happy or unhappy. But how? Ask any Buddhist that same question, and they will "shrug their shoulders" and look at you with an expression of "poor westerner," needing science to prove to you something Buddhists have known for thousands of years. You don't have to be a Buddhist to practice and learn mindfulness. Attend any good yoga class or seek out learning about meditation or you may just need the information below.

"Everybody is talking about mindfulness... but nobody seems to be able to explain clearly what the heck it really is." (Barker) Again we see a mismatch in words, the language that is used by practitioners Vs. scientists involved in mindfulness. We saw the problem of language before as we bridge the gulf between technology professionals and senior management. Just as there should not be some deathmatch between technical and management, "... there isn't some looming deathmatch between mindfulness and neuroscience, between East and West. They're actually on the same page." (Barker) We see the same with the different languages used by technical professionals Vs. senior management. Research in neuroscience shows that mindfulness reduces stress, helps us focus on the present (here and now), and helps us to monitor ourselves even when we are unable to control the situation.

For our discussion and understanding, we can imagine that the human brain is divided into a Left half and a Right half. Each half of the brain views and interprets the world and its experiences that the individual is having differently than the other half. Yes, I know this is not logical, but as Mr. Spock has stated on numerous occasions, "Humans are not logical." Now, as we begin our sojourn into the two halves of the human brain, we must remember that in our day-to-day experiences we are not aware of the existence of the two halves of our brain. We happily go about thinking that there is one whole brain working away for the betterment of yourself.

First, we will continue our discussion about what each half of the brain do.

The right half is for concrete thinking. It's the Mr. Spock of Star Trek. The Joe Friday of Dragnet, "just the facts, ma'am." It's pretty annoying, you need to have the left half to add the "spice of life."

The Left half is the "stories teller; it will interpret your experiences. For creative types, it helps them see patterns, or pareidolia, that more right brain individuals do not see. Research done by Gazzaniga in the 1970s point to the fact that the left half, "created explanations and reasons to help make sense of what was going on." The left half of the brain acts as the "interpreter to reality," (Barker). It specializes in creating explanations of what is going on. The problem is the left side of your brain is incorrect, or just wrong, many times. Usually, it feeds us inaccurate incorrect information during the most critical times or when you are under the most stress.

As Barker stated, "The problem is you don't even realize Lefty is there. You assume the voice in your head is you and that his stories are proof of rock-solid reality." And the buzzer sounds with a resounding WRONG. You can never turn off the left half story teller, but you can say to yourself, STOP, get a grip on the situation. What is really happening here?

You have to stop ruminating and nail down the reality of the situation. You have to help the left half retell the story more correctly, actually, and with positivity interpretation.

Here is an example from the literature of what happens when a stereotypical left brain run amok; "You are sitting around a table, everyone at the table is frowning. They're not laughing at our brilliant jokes". This is a typical right brain factual reflection of the meeting. The facts, just the facts. But there is no feeling, understanding, interpretation of the meeting. Now, what does the Left half of the brain do? It does this; "Obviously, they hate us and are plotting our death."

You have to take control of both halves of your brain. Correct the facts, and rectify the interpretation. Another example is from the Nazi death camps of World War II. Two prisoners are taken to a death camp. Both physically survive the camp; one continues with life, the other is a wreck of a human never able to thrive again. Study of these two individuals shows that it was the interruptions of the situations that affected them. Classic Left brain is ruling the Right brain.

How do we take control of the situation of the left brain spiraling out of control, and telling you that everything is disastrous? How do you direct the left brain to tell a better story? How do you create a "positive feedback loop" using Neuroscience?

First, you have to tell the left brain to get a grip, then have the right brain lay out the facts. Now for a third factor, your behavior! Change your behavior, and you will change your emotion. This is a technique taken from cognitive behavioral therapy. By physically doing something you will stop the left brain downward spiral and start the upward spiral that you want. Next, write down your new story you will be amazed at how much better you feel, how much better your meeting will go.

The next section will help you control the left brain by listening to what another person is actually saying, not just responding to them but understand them.

Listening to Understand not just to Reply

What is one of the hardest issue you deal every day? Listening! Unfortunately, most people don't listen to understand the person; they only listen to immediately reply to what the other person has said, or what we think they have said.

> **The biggest issue in communicating is that we don't listen to comprehend**
>
> **We listen to reply immediately.**

A study was conducted at Princeton University by Charles G. Gross in 2010 where they found that "there is a lag between what you hear and what you understand." (Eklund) It is this lag-time where the problems in communication begin. We start to listen to ourselves, our brain starts interpreting the partial information, and our comprehension plummets. Research is showing that one of the chief causes of our lack of knowledge and understanding is the "confirmation bias," which is the tendency to lock onto facts or parts of the conversation that confirm the listener's existing beliefs, values, or perceptions. Eklund states "You're only listening to what you want to hear." So, again a classical definition of a cognitive bias of being the tendency to search for or interpret information in a way that confirms one's preconceptions can be modified to fit an individual situation.

When engaged in listening, the brain is not using its complete potential. The brain is always fully active, but when it is only partial being utilized, listening, the other areas of the brain will begin to drifts off in multiple directs all at the same time.

An interesting phenomenon in the field of "listening to understand" is called Miller's Law. This is based on research conducted in 1980 that states in order to understand what another person is saying, you have to assume that the speaker's statement is true.

Listening as if the speaker's statements are right allow these statements to enter your brain unaltered. Now, you can start analyzing the statements formulating a positive professional response that shows you understood and not just giving a "knee-jerk" reaction.

In closing our discussion on "listening to understand" Let review a modified list of Eklund's 7 suggestions for better listening.

Listening to Understand

1. Get rid of outside distractions

- [ ] Put everything down that includes your phone.
- [ ] Close the outside world, that includes glancing at your computer;s email.
- [ ] Breathe slowly and deeply; listening is difficult to get into the zone
- [ ] Physically relax and get comfortable. If you are in a comfortable, you won't be fidgeting.
- [ ] Detail notes are a listening killer
  - [ ] I remember in undergraduate school our professor told us to put your pencil down and just listen to what she had to say. That was a mind changing experience.
  - [ ] Most people hear what is being said, but they don't listen to what is being said.

Listening to Understand

2. Open your mind

- [ ] Don't judge, Only listen
  - [ ] Judging a person as he is speaking is another listening killer
- [ ] Repeat what the person is saying in your head
  - [ ] Just the highlights, not details
  - [ ] You may discover that the person is saying something smart, meaningful, and intelligent

Listening to Understand

3. Listen to the big picture, not the details.

- [ ] Look for the path that the speaker is going down not the rocks, mud, limbs that will distract you.
    - [ ] Get the overall purpose of the speaker message, so you are not distracted.
    - [ ] Get their overall point, so you are not distracted.
- [ ] Don't listen competitively
    - [ ] Don't argue, in your mind, with the speaker.
    - [ ] Yes, this is natural, especially if the point of view differs from yours

Listening to Understand

4. As you listen notice the speaker nonverbal communications

- [ ] Rule 1 about observing nonverbal communication
    - [ ] Don't get all wrapped up in it.
    - [ ] Use multiples of the items listed below to reinforce your understanding
        - [ ] How are they sitting, standing, etc.?
        - [ ] How's the eye contact?
        - [ ] Is their speech fast or slow, smooth or broken?
        - [ ] What aren't they saying?
        - [ ] How is their presentation? Are they using Vividness effect
            - Are you being drawn in because of the speaker's sensational, vivid, or memorable delivery, not the speaker's substances?
            - Are they using personal

testimony?
- ☐ There often trumps evidence or higher reliability
- To counter the vividness effect repeat the speaker words in your head to give you focus.

Listening to Understand

5. Do not jump to conclusions or interrupt.

☐ Don't interrupt the speaker let them complete their thought
  - ☐ In Between, sentences ask for clarification or ask the speaker to repeat they're important points.
  - ☐ By asking to clarify questions, this will reduce the vividness effect.
☐ You have done the opposite from what the speaker expected.
  - ☐ You did not interrupt them
  - ☐ You take a few moments or longer to think about your response before you response
  - ☐ The speaker will be surprised, shocked, distrustful, "thrown off their game" because you didn't immediately respond to them
    - ☐ Because of the speaker shock to your behavior, you will need to tell them that you were thinking about what they were saying.
    - ☐ A standard technique is to paraphrase back to the speaker what they just statement, not like a parrot but in your

words. This proves you were really listening and attempting to understand the meaning of the speaker point of view.

- ☐ The goal of this approach is to increase good decision making by slowing down the decision process and enhance the understanding of the decision.

Listening to Understand
6. Understand the essence of what the speaker is saying.
- ☐ Let the speaker know you heard him, by using the techniques below
    - ☐ Paraphrasing
    - ☐ Repeat key points
    - ☐ Don't add emotions
    - ☐ Don't speak from your perspective
    - ☐ Stay Focus

Listening to Understand
7. Challenge yourself first.
- ☐ As Miller stated in his research; challenge yourself, think in terms that the speaker statements could be true.
    - ☐ Challenge yourself to think under what situation can the speaker message be true.
    - ☐ Try to understand the person
        - ☐ "You can understand a person, without agreeing with them."
- ☐ Be non-confrontational
    - ☐ You seek to understand the speaker's message

> ☐ Ask non-challenging question,
> ☐ Ask questions to understand.

Practice, Practice and Practice your listening skills with friends, family, strangers. Listening skills can be learned and are powerful tools. Attend workshops on listening, mindfulness, and Assertiveness (non-confrontational) skills. Then add those skills to your understanding of cognitive biases and social engineering giving you greater potential in marketing and selling security, or any other product.

Now that we have examined the neuroscience of mindfulness and the art of listening it is time to return to cognitive biases and how they affect decision making. How can we use these cognitive biases to our advantage and avoiding letting them be a stumbling block to our working with senior management?

We have found numerous cognitive biases that can have an effect on decision making and we are going to discuss a few of them on the following pages. A couple of useful articles to read are: "Avoiding Psychological Bias in Decision Making" and "The 12 Cognitive biases that prevent you from being rational".

1. Confirmation Bias

The classic definition of Confirmation bias is: "The tendency to search for, interpret, focus on and remember information in a way that confirms one's preconceptions." by Oswald and Grosjean in 2004.

In this chapter, we are interested in applying this cognitive bias to decision making. You will remember that this configuration bias happens when you look for information that supports your existing beliefs and reject data that go against what you believe. This can lead you to make biased decisions because you didn't factor in all of the relevant information.

A 2013 study at Yale University found that the way people view statistics is affected by confirmation bias. The authors reported that people have a tendency to infer information from statistics that support their existing beliefs, even when the data support an opposing view, a stereo-classic confirmation bias description. Because so many decisions in business is based on statistical data, the confirmation bias can create a grave and potentially costly mistake.

Putting it to use:
One of the best technique to challenge any cognitive bias and confirmational bias, in particular, is to seek out information from a range of sources, not just your favorites. Go and find an opposing point of view. You will be able to combat the confirmation bias by understanding the opposite point of view.

Another technique is to develop a diverse group of friends, and co-workers so are willing to discuss divergent viewpoints. Practice your listening skills by truly listening to dissenting views. Remember, a standard approach is to hear the opposing argument as if it was true.

Finally, if you are working with a team appoint someone to be the devil's advocate for major decisions. It is their job to research opposing facts, to formulate an argument that supports a different strategy. This approach is also known as the 10th Man Rule.

Anchoring
This bias is the tendency to jump to conclusions. Base your final judgment on information gained early on in the decision-making process. Think of this as a "first impression" bias. Once you form an initial

picture of a situation, it's hard to see other possibilities.

Putting it to use:

A common way that the Anchoring bias clouds our decision-making process are when you feel under pressure to make a quick decision, or if you have a general tendency to act impulsively. Think of the sale person who throws out a price point, then quickly move to other options. They have planted the original price in your brain. Always lead with the price or the options that you want the decision makers to pick. Then use a decoy that readily supports the anchor.

So, how do you avoid the Anchoring bias? Reflect on your decision-making history and think about whether you've rushed to judgment in the past. Now, take the time to make decisions slowly, analyze the fact, weigh the pros and cons of the decision choices, use the Ben Franklin process. Be prepared to ask for longer if you feel under pressure to make a quick decision. If someone is pressing for a quick decision, then this can be a clear sign that they're pushing for a decision that is against your best interests.

Use the "Ladder of Inference" to discover the stages of thinking that individuals and/or groups progress through to make good decisions.

Ladder of Inference
1. Facts.
2. Interpreted Reality.
3. Conclusions.
4. Beliefs.
5. Action.
6. Decision.

Overconfidence Bias

Ever been wrong, even when you thought you were right. This happens when you place too much faith in your own knowledge, opinions, or past history. You may also believe that your contribution to a decision is more valuable than it actually is. You may be the pivotal person or the keystone in decision making, but that doesn't make your decision correct.

Many times we can combine overconfidence bias with the anchoring bias. Under this combination, people act on hunches and have an unrealistic view of their decision-making ability. With a little pressure and encouragement, stroking of our ego, the target can be pressed in a bad decision.

In a study conducted by Simon, Houghton, and Aquiro they found that entrepreneurs are more likely to display the overconfidence bias than the general population. Entrepreneurs perceive a venture as less risky because they are unable to identify their limited knowledge of a particular subject area. This overconfidence bias has doomed many a venture.

Putting it to use:
Whether you are using the overconfidence bias or combatting the overconfidence consider the following questions in your decision making:

Overconfidence Questions
☐ What is your information sources?
☐ Which ones do you rely on in decision making?
☐ Are the sources fact-based or hunches by an "expert".?
☐ How do you gather information; Who is involved
☐ Are the sole source for gathering information?
☐ Are other involved in gathering information?
☐ Do they think just like you?
☐ Do you use a systematical approach to gather information
☐ Do you include multiple sources?
☐ Do you include both pro and con sources?
☐ Do you have a trusted agents that will be your "devil

advocate." Also known as the 10th Man Rule.
- ☐ Will they challenge you?
- ☐ Will they put forward alternatives?

Think about your team, did they gather comprehensive and objective data. Guard yourself and your team against depending on the unreliable information.

Gambler's Fallacy

Do you believe that past random events will influence the future, if so then you could fall victim to the gambler's fallacy? This fallacy was first attributed to Laplace's essay of 1796, so documenting people's beliefs that past random events will influence the future has been studied for a long time. A classic example is a coin toss. If you toss a coin and get heads seven times consecutively, you might assume that there's a higher chance that you'll toss head the eighth time.

On the opposite side of the coin, pud intended, the longer the series, the stronger you began to believe that the next toss of the coin will produce different results. "Thing has got to change." We all know that the odds are always 50/50 is a coin toss.

Why is the gambler's fallacy so dangerous in decision making? Imagine you're working with someone who makes investment in a highly volatile market. They have had a half dozen successes in a row. You, like them, see a pattern of success. Humans are always looking for and finding patterns, even when there are none. This is an excellent example of how we think that the number of successes in the past with a volatile subject will produce positive results in the future. The outcome is highly still uncertain.

Putting it to use:
If you wish to use or combat the gambler's fallacy, consider reading the following research from the Harvard School of Business. In their study, it was noted that decisions were based on how the information was acquired. Analysis suggests that the way information is encountered will determine whether or not predictions exhibit the gambler's fallacy

It has also been reported that the gambler's fallacy was less likely to happen when decision makers avoided looking at information chronologically. To help prevent the gambler's fallacy, look at trends, patterns, from a number of angles. Use tools that will allow you to drill deep into the data.

Watch for patterns in behavior or product. Do they have success or failure? Look beyond the data look at the environment, changing customer's preferences or economic circumstances.

Fundamental Attribution Error
When something is successful, it was my personality, my abilities. When something fails, it's everyone else's fault. What happens when a project fails, does leadership look objectively at the situation or do they blame others. Are people accused or judged based on a stereotype or perceived personality flaw.

For example, if you're in an automobile accident, and the other driver is at fault, you're more likely to assume that he or she is a bad driver than you are to consider whether inclement weather played a role. Now, think about the project that failed. Did you come to the same conclusion as the automobile accident stated above?

Putting it to use:

The best way to avoid the Fundamental Attribution Error in decision making is to look at the situation, not the people involved. Use empathy in conducting a post momentum of the project. Increase your understand of people by developing cultural intelligence, to understand why people behave the way that does. And your own emotional intelligence which will allow you to reflect on your personal behavior more accurately.

The following is a quick list of other cognitive biases and their definitions that can affect decision making. For more details, the authors recommend checking the following sources; "list of Cognitive Biases" in Wikipedia, Dvorsky's article "The 12 Cognitive Biases that Prevent you from Being Rational", and The Sales Psychology Toolkit by Addison.

- ☐ Bandwagon effect
    - ☐ The tendency to do (or believe) things because many other people do (or believe) the same.
- ☐ Current Moment Bias
    - ☐ We, humans, have a tough time imagining ourselves in the future and altering our behaviors and expectations accordingly. Most of

us would rather experience pleasure in the current moment while leaving the pain for later.

☐ **Ingroup Bias**
    ☐ A pattern of favoring members of one's in-group over the out-group members. This can be expressed in evaluation of others, in the allocation of resources, and in many other ways. The in-group bias causes us to overestimate the abilities and value of our immediate group at the expense of people we don't really know. This is a manifestation of our innate tribalistic tendencies. Appears to have neurological basis.

☐ **Negativity Bias**
    ☐ People tend to pay more attention to bad news. It is theorized that this is a reaction to our selective attention. In addition, we perceive negative news as being more important or profound.

☐ **Observational Selection Bias**

☐ This is an effect of suddenly noticing things we hadn't notice before but because we are now noticing, seeing, that thing now we assume that the frequency has increased. They are wrongfully believing that the rate has increased when in reality we are incorrect.

☐ Projection Bias

☐ We tend to assume that most people think just like us. This is a false consensus bias in which we believe that people think like us and agree with us. We assume that there exists a consensus when there may be none.

☐ Status Quo

☐ We, humans, tend to be apprehensive of change, which often leads us to make choices that guarantee that things remain the same, or change as little as possible. "If it ain't broke, don't fix it."

Test Yourself - Test your Team

How do you minimize the impact of cognitive biases? How do you maximize the impact of cognitive biases? You can test yourself and your team by asking the following three questions to determine if you are under the influence of a Cognitive Bias.

Minimizing Cognitive Biases

☐ Is your team guilty of self-interest, overconfidence, or attachment to past experiences?

☐ Did your team fall in love with your recommendation?

☐ Is your team guilty of groupthink?

In Conclusion

Let's review the keys of this chapter on conflict resolution, problem-solving, and decision making. There is much to learn about surviving the business world that us geeks did learn in school. You must learn to speak the language of business. You must learn to make your mind happy, by practicing "Mindfulness," focusing on the "here and how" on the positive even in a bad situation, on seeing the world from the senior manager point of view. To help you achieve this, you must practice listening to understand.

Why should you care or learn mindfulness? Research in neuroscience has shown that using the techniques and skills of mindfulness reduces stress, help us focus on the present situation and problem and help guide us in controlling ourselves, our responses when we cannot control the outcome of the situation.

Another key point of this chapter is how our brain is divided into a left, storyteller, interprets side and concrete, just the facts side. That we must learn to control our left side from running away with fanciful, illogical, and unreality ideas, beliefs, and conclusions. We discussed how you must practice your listening skills daily which in turn will help you with you interruptive skills, balancing the left and right halves of your brain.

To continue, we examine several cognitive biases that directly affect decision making including; confirmation bias, Anchoring, Overconfidence, Gambler's Fallacy, and several more with examples of "putting them into practice."

We ended this chapter by asking you several cognitive biases reduced to simple questions.

These will make easy references for your presentations to management.

Social Engineering (People Hacking):

Using the combination of social engineering techniques and cognitive biases you can create an impressive sales presentation. In this section, we will discuss what is social engineering and then refer back it to the section in Marketing, Sales, and Decision Making of examples.

Hackers are not the only people to use social engineering methods; head-hunters, sales people and more, are becoming 'social engineers,' extracting the information they need from unwitting targets, customers, employees,etc., whose first goal is to get their job done with the minimum hassle. (changingmind.org)

An excellent source for social engineering information and practice is the Social Engineering Framework which is a searchable information resource for individuals wanting to investigate more about the history and psychology of social engineering. More and more any Business Psychology website or journal will have articles and discussions on how to use social engineering techniques.

Social engineering, in the context of information security, refers to psychological manipulation of people into performing actions or divulging confidential information. A type of confidence trick for the purpose of information gathering, fraud, or system access, it differs from a traditional "con" in that it is often one of many steps in a more complex scheme.

From the literature we learn that; All social engineering techniques are based on specific attributes of human decision-making known as cognitive biases. These biases, sometimes called "bugs in the human hardware," are exploited in various combinations to create attack techniques, some of which are listed in this text. The attacks used in social engineering can be used to obtain employees' confidential information that can assist in marketing and sales.

The most common type of social engineering happens over the phone, but for the purpose of this text, we are interested in face-to-face techniques of social engineering in a sales and marketing arena.

Mike Murr published an article where he discussed the "10 principles of successful social engineering;" we will use some of these principles listed below as the basis for our discussion in this section. Check out the URL in the references for his original article.

Social Engineering Increases The Likelihood Of Compliance

While Murr's first principle stated what social engineering couldn't do, his second principle tells you what it can do. Despite the fact that you can't force compliance, social engineering is still highly effective. This is because social engineering tactics increase the likelihood of conformity.

Murr stated the goal of a social engineer is to construct an environment that enhances the likelihood of compliance. "Everybody has their trigger, said Bruce M. Snell, director of technical marketing at McAfee Security Systems. A good social engineer will find that trigger" (O'Harrow).

Emotions Motivate Behavior

Emotion is the key to increasing the likelihood of compliance. Compliance for us is performing the desired behavior. Emotions are the motivating force behind the action and provide the goals that shape and direct our decisions.

Analyze how social engineering skills, tactics, interactions, and body language affect emotions, provides revealing perspective on what is really going on with our target and helps us learn their triggers.

Emotions Are Based On Physical States
Since emotions provide motivation for our behavior, it's important to understand what it means to experience an emotion. Murr states in his article that, while there is no standard model for emotion, there is a particular theory that several social engineers, neuroscientists, and psychologists believe ties social engineering with emotions. This theory is called Conceptual-Act Model of Emotion (C.A.M.E.).

The fundamental concept of C.A.M.E. is that the experience and how we label an emotion is based on how we interpret our core affective state, using our knowledge and understanding of the emotion, situation, and pressure we have put upon ourselves. Physically turn up the heat, introduce an irritating noise like an alarm going off behind a locked door. Add more pressure of senior management standing and looking exasperated as you try to remember the combination to unlock the door. Your interruption of the situation will determine how well you deodorant will work, today.

Under this theory for example; the cognitive bias of Framing would become a keystone of social engineering. As Murr said "Changing the frame changes the context, which changes our interpretation, and consequently our experience."

Affect Emotions, Affect Behavior

As the title implies this principle is a natural flow from the previous principle, Emotions Are Based On Physical States. If you can influence the source of behavior, then you can change the behavior itself. Many people say that this principle is evident, but not to us Geeks, think the show Big Bang Theory". This why the better social engineering, tend to be "People Person" and in most cases, not the best technical hackers.

What follows is a typical example used every day in the business world. It is called "emotional transference." The social engineering, or salesperson, or manager wants to give you the problem, or colloquially "put the monkey on your back" and only through compliances can you relieve the negative emotions.

We will combine this technique and the Principles of Sympathy and Authority. For more details read number 4 and 5 in Principles for the Science of Persuasion further in the text. People tend to compliance quick as they wish to decrease negative emotion and increase positivity ones. It is the Social Engineer skills that can create the emotion that compliance is a positivity one. This will allow us to Segways nicely into the next principle.

Psychological Hedonism For Emotions
This principle can just be stated that we seek out pleasure and one of the vast pleasure in pleasing others, especially our bosses, co-workers, lovers, etc. Under this principle, we make decisions based on the goals of minimizing pain and maximizing pleasure."

So, our approach is to put the target in a negative, a painful, situation. You have given them the "Monkey." The target is now in pain to get back to equilibrium they will comply with our request. We will now have the opportunity to reward the target with positive reinforcement causing them to feel pleasure and are more likely to help you in the future.

Emotions Provide The Motivation, Not The Solution

Read any social engineering text on utilizing emotions in "people hacking, " and you will read a statement similar to Murr's "<u>emotions are one-half of the social engineering puzzle</u>..."

As any salesperson will tell you; You must map the path to success for the customer! We must provide the goals the target's (customer's) behavior should be. Tell them what the goal is and how to get there. To create the illusion of a Win-Win, the social engineer must develop a series of desired incentives, so the target is totally aware when they have achieved the desired behavior. Any good salesperson does the same.

Associate Emotional Goals With Compliance

Social engineering is a highly successful tool used to hack individuals or organization. It is equally successful in marketing and sales. It is exponentially more powerful and fruitful when we tie it to various cognitive biases.

Many times you have heard the saying "Can't fix stupid." Social engineering works because it targets a vulnerable part of cyberspace that cannot be patched with technical fixes: human beings. (O'Harrow). Joseph Nye said, "Because it goes at the human level, not at the technological level, we're all vulnerable."

Numerous cognitive biases are tied to the concept of the target; whether the customer or senior management. It is their perception, not yours that you have to understand and cognitive biases will help. Below are just a few to help you use your Social Engineering skills.

Bandwagon Bias: Remember that this is the tendency to do or believe an action or behavior because other people are doing the same. Groupthink, a subset of the Bandwagon Bias, is one of the most powerful tools is the Social Engineer arsenal. If you are trying to use social engineering techniques get the target believing that everyone is doing the behavior you want, in a team attack situation get the SE group agreeing, adding pressure on the target to conform with the group, now you have engaged groupthink. If you are trying to counter the Bandwagon or Groupthink, use the 10th Man Rule.

Blind Spot Bias: The tendency to see oneself as less biased than other people, or to be able to identify more cognitive biases in others than in oneself.

Confirmation Bias: Confirmation Bias is the tendency to search for or interpret information in a way that confirms one's preconceptions

Overconfidence Bias: The Overconfidence Bias leads us to have more confidence than we should, given the facts. As a side point; Individual who exhibit the overconfidence bias are of the easiest to hypnotize.

Stereotyping: Expecting a member of a group to have certain characteristics without having actual information about that individual.

All the cognitive bias discussed or illustrated in this text can be used in social engineering.

In Conclusion

We are closing this section with several lists that should help you understand and use social engineering techniques in person-to-person interaction.

Our first list is by Victor Lustig who developed a set of instructions known as the "Ten Commandments for Con Men" Don't know who Victor Lustig was look here;
https://en.wikipedia.org/wiki/Victor_Lustig

Ten Commandments for Con Men

- ☐ Be a patient listener (it is this, not fast talking, that gets a con man his coups).
- ☐ Never look bored.
- ☐ Wait for the other person to reveal any political opinions, then agree with them.
- ☐ Let the other person reveal religious views, then have the same ones.
- ☐ Hint at sex talk, but don't follow it up unless the other person shows a strong interest.
- ☐ Never discuss illness, unless some special concern is shown.
- ☐ Never pry into a person's personal circumstances (they'll tell you all eventually).
- ☐ Never boast - just let your importance be quietly obvious.
- ☐ Never be untidy.
- ☐ Never get drunk.

To continue our summary, we have included the 6 principles behind the Science of Persuasion from Robert Cialdini, a social psychologist. These principles apply equally as well to Marketing, Sales or Social Engineering. For more in-depth study of his work go to
Influence: The Psychology of Persuasion

Principles of the Science of Persuasion

Principle #1: "Reciprocity.
If a request is preceded by an unexpected gift, it has greater potential to convince potential customers. The most typical example of applying this principle in marketing is "free sample." Know why we want to influence them, and what exactly those people want. This will help you implement the principle successfully.

Principle #2: "Commitment and Consistency."
Human beings have a tendency to want to appear consistent this principle can explain why it's easier to keep a customer than attract a new one.

Principle #3: "Social Proof."
When we feel uncertain about making a decision, we observe what others are doing. It's

easier to do wrong with the masses than to turn around and face the masses and tell the truth." (Keynes) Acting as society or culture expects will equal acceptance. Human tend to follow the trends of culture.

Principle #4: "Sympathy/Like-ability."

We are more likely to be influenced by the people who we like. This can be as superficial as the physical appearance of a person. In using this principle speak the same language as your customer. The customer will feel represented by you whether you talk in a Business language or Techno Babble, learn to mimic your customer. This applies to dressing in a way that's aligned with your customers and copying their body language.

Principle #5: "Authority."

People, in general, have a tendency to obey authority figures, even if those authority figures are questionable. If an authority figure or a leader in field has made a positive comment about your product or service, make it known. This will increase your sales, social engineering effort, etc.

Principle #6: "Scarcity."

People have to know what they're going to miss if they don't act quickly. Things are more attractive when their availability is limited, or when we risk losing the opportunity to acquire them. If you sell a product and there are only a few items left, make it known to the customer or you social engineering target. People will want to buy our product or share information ever more. Another trick is to limit the number of units a person make have. Humans buy more when we know we can <u>not</u> buy more.

As we close out our Social Engineering discussion let's look at psychological tricks that you can use to get your Target to like you. These are based on an article by several individuals plus our life experiences and research in interpersonal relations.

Copy your target's behavior and mannerisms. Called mirroring effect. Subtly, not obviously copy the target's body language, gestures, facial expressions, the pronunciation of words. Not their accent, but selected words. Example if they don't use a contraction like I just wrote, you could also use the word "do not." Subtly, unnoticeable behavior that only the target's subconscious would pick.

Spend time around your target. Called mere-exposure effect. Humans are predictable animals they like the status quo, items that are familiar to them. Several studies have shown that only spending more time with your target will make them like you more than individuals they don't spend time with.

Compliment your target and others associated with them. Called spontaneous trait transferences. This is not "Kissing Up" to your Target, although there is a time and place for that in social engineering. Humans love a good compliment especially if it is done in front of Target's peers. Complementing the Target communicate positive emotions and make them feel happy and positive.

Be in a great mood around your target. Called emotional contagion. This is a follow-on of the above statement. Humans are influenced to a large degree by the moods of other people. Every notice that one sour apple can spoil a barrel of apples, the same applies to a room or group of individuals. Have you ever been in a group when one person inners and the group dynamite changes from positive to negative. This effect can go the other direction when Mr. or Ms. Sunshine walks into a room. Your target can unconsciously feel the emotions of those around them, communicate positive emotions and they will want you in the inner circle of the decision makers.

Make friends with the Target's friends. Called triadic closure from social-network theory. Combine this with the art of acting as if you like the target. Called reciprocity of liking. Social media is a good start. Having lunch with the group is another tactic. Now , add a third trick and emphasize your shared values this is known as a similarity-attraction effect. Here the old saying "Birds of a feather" applies. Did you and the target go to the same high school, or college, or grow up in the same town or community. Did you play similar sports, band, like the same genre of music? Like the same sports teams. Are you involved in same or comparable exercise like running or swimming, scouts or volunteer for a charity?

Everyone loves a compliment, but when they are contentious, they lost their power. So don't be complimentary all the time gauge when and how much positive reinforcement you should provide your Target. For more information read more about the gain-loss theory and under Behavioral Psychology read about B.F. Skinner's Operant Conditioning Intermittent Reinforcement.

Want your target to feel like they can trust you? Then be warm, smile and seem competent in your field. A winning smile and friendly attitude are first signs that demonstrate that you are competent in your field but not a threat to the target. The target will judge you based on stereotype content modeling.

The pratfall effect is a phenomenon that suggests that your target will have a perceived positive attraction to you if you make simple mistakes if you show a flaw. Maybe you are clumsy, absent-minded, wear mismatched clothes, or like me your wear bow ties.

Human touch is one of the most powerful tool/skill/weapon in the toolkit for social engineers. In psychology we would use the subliminal touch, which is barely noticeable but registers positivity in the target's brain, to increase a warm feeling to you. This is a sample, just a tap on the back or a light, gentle touch on the arm. Notice how people shake hands, a quick or slow, touching or the politician double hand shake. An example is a trick that wait staff has known for years, that brief touch to the customer significantly improve tips.

Everyone has a belief about themselves, an inner picture of have they view themselves, their action, their world-view. This is the self-verification theory in action, and people want to be perceived in a way that aligns with their view of themselves. The target will interact with those individuals who give feedback that is consistent with their identity.

"Laugh and the World laugh with you, cry ..." people want to be around persons with a sense of humor, studies after studies state that it is important. Add to a sense of humor displaying caring, fairness, and using the target's name and you have a winning combination.

People love to talk about themselves whether a person is talking in front of another people or just to themselves the motivation and reward regions in the brain was active telling us that talking about yourself is rewarding. Let the target tell their stories, their little anecdote; they will like you for letting them do it.

Practice, Practice, and Practice

My high school and university band directors were right. Go home and practice. We must do the same with a presentation to senior management. Need I say more!

In Summary

This book started out as a reaction to numerous meetings that I have sat in and noticed that two different factions were communicating pass one another, as if the attendees were from various worlds, speaking different languages, and unable to find common ground.

In most cases, senior management wanted, needed, a quick positive response to their requirements, but the answer they got was; 1. No, and, 2. Details on why it couldn't be done, in other words; "how to make a watch."

I think that we have outlined in this text several successful ways in which security, or any technical staff, can successfully communicate with senior management and develop a Win-Win solution to the increasingly balancing act.

We must work as a team to improve profits and security at the same time. It is technologist job to develop a successful roadmap to help management win while at the same time prospecting company and national assets.

If you enjoyed this book, we would like to call your attention to our other books.

For more example, samples, and discussion see our next book coming out in late 2017 entitled <u>Social Engineering: A Practioner Guide</u>.

Sampling of Slides used in our Presentations and Workshops

Winning Management Buy-In to Security

SA and TE Hale
PhreakNIK 2016

SA and Terry Hale

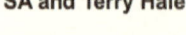

How do we as security professionals plead our case to vice presidents, senior management, and stakeholders that security issues are real and imminent dangers? h

Convincing the King that He's Not Invisible to Dragons

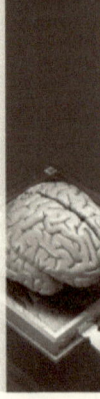

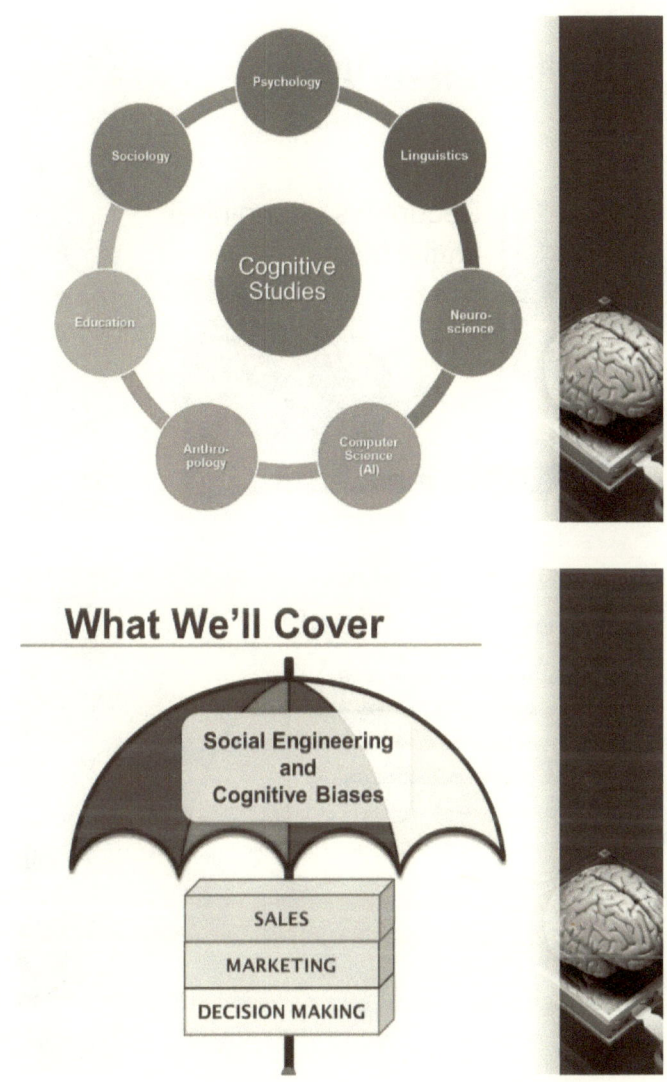

What We'll Cover

Social Engineering
and
Cognitive Biases

SALES

MARKETING

DECISION MAKING

Selling Security

Security is intangible...
until it fails.

How do you sell an intangible?
How do you sell failure?

What's Important

❖ Senior Management buy-in to security is vital
   for the success of our security endeavors.
❖ For years there has been this tendency to understate the
   impact when an incident occurs.
❖ The decision makers must have an understanding of the
   importance of a strong cyber-security program.
❖ Mitigation must be made proactive.

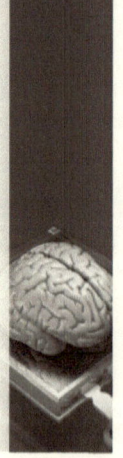

What's Important

> I hate when it's dark and my brain is like, "Hey, you know what we haven't thought about in a while? **Monsters.**"

- ❖ Don't tell them how to build the watch when all they wanted was the time.
- ❖ Learn to talk to managers and decision makers.
- ❖ Market and sell security using cognitive biases and social engineering.

Anthropology

- ❖ Think of yourself as an anthropologist.
- ❖ You're venturing into and exploring a strange, unusual culture – foreign to your Geekdom.
- ❖ You'll need to learn new ways to speak and act.
- ❖ The success of your mission depends on your action.

Why Computer Security is Good Business

The biggest issue in communicating
is that we don't
listen to comprehend.

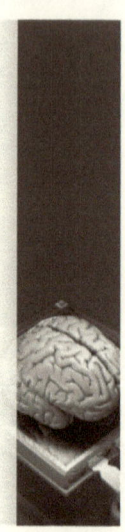

We listen to
reply immediately.

Listen to Understand

1. Get rid of outside distractions.
2. Open your mind.
3. Listen for the big picture, not the details.
4. Watch for nonverbal communications.
5. Do not jump to conclusions
   or interrupt.
6. Understand the essence
   of what the speaker is saying.
7. Challenge yourself first.

Ladder
of Inference

This is the subconscious thinking process we go through to get from a fact to a decision.

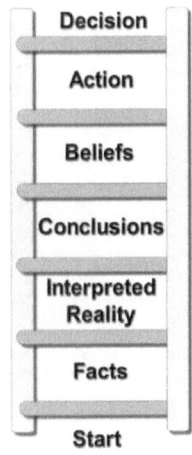

From Organization Psy.Chris Argyris, Peter Senge:
The Fifth Discipline: The Art and Science of the Learning Organization

Ladder of Inference

Scott attends a team meeting. When he brings up an idea to improve work flow, another employee sighs and says, "Let's move on." The discussion shifts and Scott's idea is ignored.

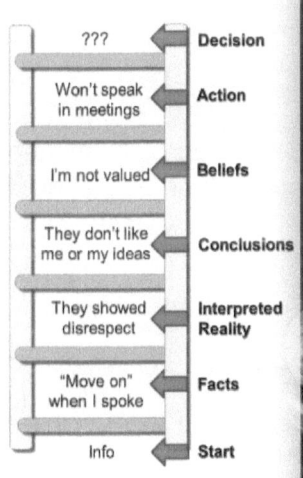

Simple Goals

Change this graphic

1	• Educate
2	• Create a team
3	• Engage
4	• Promote

Three Questions

- Is your team guilty of self-interest, overconfidence, or attachment to past experiences?
- Has your team fallen in love with your recommendation?
- Is your team guilty of groupthink?

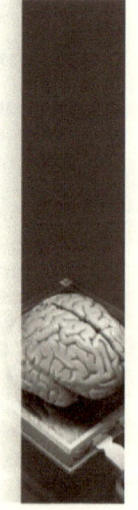

Communication

- Write a script – but don't memorize
- Open with your conclusions, including costs
- What is most important to your audience?
- Use questions to empower
- Make eye contact

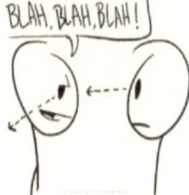

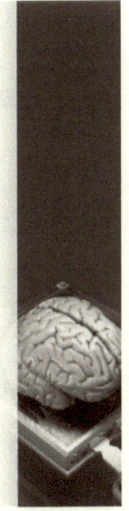

Communication

- Practice your message
- Tell time, not how to make the watch
- Tell your story, your way
- Have backup
- Stay on, or under, time

Ikea Effect

How many of you have shopped at Ikea? Takes a long time, lots To see. Then get the items to your vehicle, get it home, and then Assemble.

In experiment, subjects put together a 2 for $10 Ikea storage box. After the experiment, they were offered either the box they built Or one that was already put together by experts. They invariably Chose the one they built.

Another experiment – subjects weren't told the price of the piece Of furniture they built. When asked how much they'd pay for it, The average price was 63% more than the catalog price.

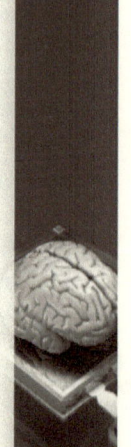

Ambiguity Effect

The Ambiguity Effect is basically a fear of the unknown.

A bird in the hand. . .

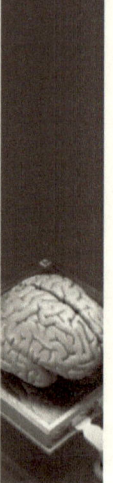

Confirmation Bias

Confirmation Bias is the tendency to search for or interpret information in a way that confirms one's preconceptions

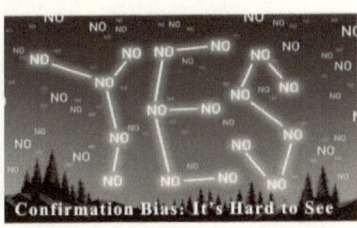

Confirmation Bias: It's Hard to See

"I meant to do that."
For example, people who support or oppose a particular issue will not only seek information that supports their beliefs, they will also interpret news stories in a way that upholds their existing ideas and remember things in a way that also reinforces these attitudes.

SOCIAL ENGINEERING
The clever manipulation of the natural human tendency to trust.

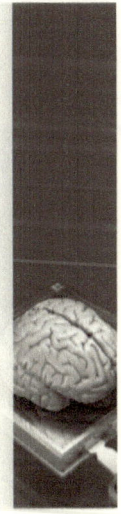

Social Engineering

- ❖ Social Engineering is a very successful tool used in hacking, marketing, and sales.
- ❖ Emotion is key to increasing the likelihood of compliance.
- ❖ Cognitive Bias of Framing is a keystone of social engineering.
- ❖ If you can affect the source of a behavior, you can affect the actual behavior.
- ❖ One of the greatest pleasures is pleasing others, especially our work team.
- ❖ To be successful, there must be an awareness of the desired behavior.

Social Engineering

Social Engineering works because it targets a vulnerable part of cyberspace that cannot be patched with technical fixes: **Human Beings**.

10 Commandments...
for Con Men

❖ Be a patient listener.

❖ Never look bored.

❖ Wait for the other person
to reveal any political opinions, then agree with them.

❖ Let the other person reveal religious views,
then agree with them.

❖ Hint at sex talk, but don't follow it up unless
the other person shows a strong interest.

*Victor Lustig (1890-1947),
professional con man

References:

Addison, Matt (2016). <u>The Sales Psychology Toolkit</u> Amazon Digital Services LLC

Ady, Wendy E. (2001). <u>Secure This: Organizational Buy-in</u>. SANS Institute InfoSec Reading Room

Altman, Morris (2012). <u>Behavioral Economics for Dummies.</u> Mississauga, ON Wiley

Anderson, Jim & James Chambers. (2011 July 08). <u>Security Business Cases: Fact and Fiction in Selling Security</u>. RSA Conference 2011. YouTube. https://www.youtube.com/watch?v=5AUUK0Q1Z0A

Anderson, Mike (unknown). <u>Hacking the Mind by Understanding Biases - Ambiguity Effect</u>. http://www.mikeyanderson.com

Barker, Eric (2016). <u>How to make your mind Happy, According to Neuroscience</u>. From blog Barking Up the Wrong Tree. http://time.com/4470517/neuroscience-of-mindfulness/

Barker, Eric (2015). New Neuroscience reveals 4 rituals that will make you Happy. http://www.bakadesuyo.com/2015/09/make-you-happy-2/
From blog Barking Up the Wrong Tree.

Barreiro, Alfonso (2012). How to Sell Information Security to Management. http://techrepublic.com pages 6.

Barron, Gregory & Stephen Leider (October 16, 2008). Making the Gambler's Fallacy Disappear: The Role of Experience. Harvard Business School

Barry (2015). 10 Ways To Use Cognitive Biases To Persuade & Influence http://www.ciphr.com/blog/cognitive-biases/

Beaver, Kevin (2002) Selling Security to Upper Management. http://searchwindowsservertechnet.com

Birmingham, Andrew. (2011 October 05). 10 Tips for Talking Human for Alpha Geeks. Computerworld Australia. www.cio.com.au/article/403076/how_talk_management

Brudner, Emma (2015). How to Use Psychological Biases to Sell Better and Faster. HotSpot, https://blog.hubspot.com

Cialdini, Robert (2008) Influence Science and Practice, ePub (5th ed)

Chabris, Christopher (2010) The Invisible Gorilla

Childs, Mike (2015). Part 2: Tips to Sell Security Successfully. Page 5 https://www.rooksecurity.com/autho/mike-childsrooksecurity-com/

Cole, Eric. (2009). Network Security Bible 2nd. Wiley Publishing

Cordy, Matt. (2016). 17 Psychological Tricks To Make People Like You Immediately Business Insider. http://www.businessinsider.com/how-to-make-people-like-you-2016-4

Davis, Michael (2011). How to Sell Security Solutions without Using Fear, Uncertainty and Doubt.

Dvorsky, George (2013). The 12 Cognitive Biases that prevent You from Being Rational. Io9.
http://io9.gizmodo.com/5974468/the-most-common-cognitive-biases-that-prevent-you-from-being-rational

Jeremy Dean (2010). The Illusion of Truth. PsyBlog
http://www.spring.org.uk/2010/12/the-illusion-of-truth.php

Eklund, Andy (2014). Listening to Understand vs. Listening to reply.
www.andyeklund.com/listening-to-understand/comfirmationbias

Fripp, Patricia. Selling Yourself and Your Idea to Senior Management. Unknown.
www.fripp.com/public-speaking-selling-yourself-and-your-idea-to-senior-management

Fradin, Russ (2015). 5 Great Ways to engage Your Employees with Content Marketing.
http://www.clickz.com/5-great-ways-to-engage-your-employees-with-content-marketing/26688/ Community Management Marketing Soical Strategies.

Gebreel, Amro (2016). Tips for Selling Security.
http://www.computerweekly.com

Gill, James (2015). <u>Cognitive Bias Parade 1</u> (volume 1).
http://www.cognitivebiasparade.com

Grannema, Joseph (unknown). <u>What's the best way to sell security strategies to executives?</u> Pages 4 http://searchsecuritytecharnet.com

Hale, SA and Terry Hale (2015). <u>Cognitive Biases Affect on Security</u>. Presentation at the 2015 PhreakNIC 19, Nashville, TN. Book In work.

Johnson, M. Eric (2007). <u>Embedding Information Security into the Organization</u>. IEEE Computer Society, IEEE Security & Privacy, 1540-7993/07, pages 17-24. http://computer.org/security/

Kosutic, Djan (2012). <u>9 steps to Cybersecurity. The Manager's Information Security Strategy Manual</u>. EPPS Services Ltd, Zagreb https://iso27001standard.com

Langford, Thom. (2015 May 06). <u>Stop Selling and Start Marketing Your Information Security Program</u>. RSA Conference 2015. You Tube. https://www.youtube.com/watch?v=d4HMDs Gnm04

Leite, Adriano (2012). How to Sell the Value of Information security - The four "Rs." http://myinfosearch.com

Levitt, Steven and Stephen Dubner (2015). Think Like A Freak. First William Morrow Epub Edition.

McGlone, Matthew (2016). Sounds True to Me. Psychology Today. https://www.psychologytoday.com/articles/199809/sounds-true-me

Medina, John (2014). Brain Rules: 12 Principles for Surviving and Thriving at Work, Home, and School. Pear Press; 2 Upd Exp edition

Mind Tools editorial team (2016). How to Make Objective Decisions. www.mindtools.com/article/avioding-psychological-bias.html

Mitnick, Kevin (2002). The Art of Deception. Wiley Publishing, Inc. Indianapolis, Indiana

Murr, Mike (2016). 10 Principles for Successful Social Engineering. https://socialexploits.com/blog/10-principles-for-successful-social-engineering/ Social Exploits.

Nelson, Ray (2013). Tips for Engaging Your Employees in Company Marketing Efforts. Stan Phelps blog. http://www.ginchmarketing.com/2013/04/21/tips-for-engaging-your-employees-in-company-marketing-efforts/

O'Harrow, Robert (2012). In Cyberattacks, hacking humans is highly effective way to access systems. https://www.washingtonpost.com/investigations/in-cyberattacks-hacking-humans-is-highly-effective-way-to-access-systems/2012/09/26/2da66866-ddab-11e1-8e43-4a3c4375504a_story.html The Washington Post.

Reck, Robb (2011). Getting Buy-in for Information Security. Enterprise InfoSec Blog. pages 5. http://infosecisland.com.
Rothman, Mike (2008). How to get Information Security buy-in from the executive team. http://searchwindowsservertechnet.com

Renahan, Mike (2015). 20 Weird Cognitive Biases Influencing Your BUyer's Decision. https://blog.hubspot.com

Schneier (2016). How to Sell Security. http://Schneier.com Pages 15.

Sherizen, Sanford (2000) <u>The Business Case for Information Security: Selling Management on the Protection of Vital Secrets and Products</u>. Auerbach Publications, 82-01-32, pages 6.

Simon, Mark, Susan Houghton, Karl Aquiro (March 2000), <u>Cognitive biases, risk perception, and venture formation: How individuals decide to start companies</u> Journal of Business Venturing Volume 15, Issue 2, page 113-134
http://www.sciencedirect.com/science/article/pii/S0883902698000032

Slotosch, Andreas (2014). <u>Make Your Employees Your First and Best Customers</u>.
https://beekeeper.io/make-your-employees-your-first-and-best-customers/
Best Practice, Events

Sovezah, Art (2011). <u>Smarten Up Your Prospecting Calls with "Social Engineering"</u>
http://smartcalling.com/newsite/smarten-up-your-prospecting-calls-with-social-engineering/ Smart Calling.

Todd, David (2016). Selling Your Information Security Strategy. SANS Institute InfoSec Reading Room.

Unknown 2016. <u>Analysis of Cybersecurity Framework RFI Responses</u>. US Government publication National Institute of Standards and Technology (NIST), Applied Cybersecurity Division, Information Technology Laboratory. Pages 18.

Unknown. Social Engineering Framework. <u>Sales Peoples: Pretexting, Elicitation, Passive Information Gathering</u>. http://www.social-engineer.org/framework/general-discussion/categories-social-engineers/sales-people/

Unknown (2013). 5 Things Your Employees can do to Help Promote Your Business. http://www.amsterdamprinting.com/blog/2013/04/25/5-things-your-employees-can-do-to-help-promote-your-business

Viljoen, Tommy (2014). <u>Cyber Security Empowering the CIO</u>. <u>Deloitte CIO Cyber Security Handbook</u>. Pages 40. https://www.deloitte.com.au

Watt, George. (2009 May). <u>10 Tips for Effective Presentations to Senior Executives</u>. Innovation, Technology, and Life in the Cloud. http://pragmaticcloud.wordpress.com/when-techs-talk-to-execs

Wood, Peter. (Moderators). (2015 July 17). Articulating Risk to Senior Management Enabling Informed Decision Making. Infosecurity Europe 2015 Day Two Keynote Stage Panel. You Tube.
https://www.youtube.com/watch?v=O7b1Wf4GefM

Zorz, Mirko (2010). How to Sell Security to Senior Management.
http://www.helpnetsecurity.com

2013. 5 Things Your Employees can do to Help Promote Your Business.
http://www.amterdamprinting.com/blog/2013/04/25/5-things-your-employees-can-do-to-help-promote-your-business

About the Authors:

 Mr. Hale is a Computer Scientist with over 30 years of experience, as well as, a Cognitive Scientist with over 40 years of experience Predominantly utilizing an interdisciplinary approach that brings the human side to technology by combining Cognitive and Behavioral Science, with Computer and Security Engineering. Mr. Hale works in various areas including Security Engineering, Information Assurance, System Administration, Cyber Warfare, Cognitive System Engineering, and Software Engineering.

Mr. Hale uses the human centric computing approach during his typical day as a Cyber Technical Lead, System Administrator, and Information System Security Officer (ISSO) for several classified laboratories.

He has provided engineering and analysis support to the Missile Defense Agency (MDA), Ground-based Missile Defense (GMD), Space and Missile Defense Command (SMDC),

United States Marine Corps (USMC), United States Navy (USN), Department of Homeland Security (DHS), State of Alabama, National Guard Bureau, and other government and commercial groups both foreign and domestic.

Additionally, Mr. Hale is an Adjunct Professor of Computer Science at Athens State University where he teaches courses in System Security Management, Digital Forensics, Cyber Ethics, and Javascript.

You may contact Mr. Hale at ProfessorHale@gmail.com or AbbyNormalResearch@gmail.com

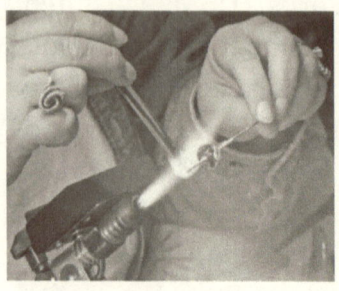

Terry Hale has been fascinated with the decision-making process since she began dealing with customers in her family's business when she was a young teen. Throughout her adult life, she has studied social engineering while working in a career that includes sales, teaching, corporate training, and NASA and Department of Defense technical support.

Currently, Terry is a full-time glass artist and jewelry designer. Her designs can be found in fine art galleries and shows throughout the southeast US. In addition to teaching in her studio, Terry regularly teaches at John C. Campbell Folk School in Brasstown NC, Appalachian Center for Craft (Tennessee Tech) in Smithville TN, and at Essence of Mulranny, County Mayo, Ireland. She depends on her study of cognitive biases while teaching and decision making while selling her artwork.

You contact Terry at terry@halefireglass.com or AbbyNormalResearch@gmail.com

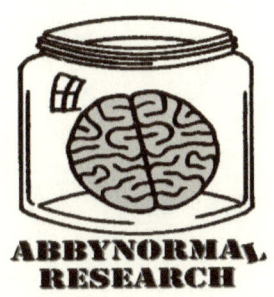

ABBYNORMAL RESEARCH

Link to our books on Amazon

Common Cognitive Biases: Examples and Challenges

https://www.amazon.com/Common-Cognitive-Biases-Examples-Challenges-ebook/dp/B0727YQSM3/ref=sr_1_1?ie=UTF8&qid=1502639336&sr=8-1&keywords=SA+Hale

Predictive Cyber Threat Analysis using Data Science: An Overview of Possibilities

https://www.amazon.com/Predictive-Cyber-Threat-Analysis-Science/dp/1546727841/ref=sr_1_2?ie=UTF8&qid=1502640151&sr=8-2&keywords=SA+Hale

Hacker Profiling: An Overview of Approaches

https://www.amazon.com/Hacker-Profiling-Overview-Approaches-Hale-ebook/dp/B071DZC8K7/ref=sr_1_6?ie=UTF8&qid=1502640151&sr=8-6&keywords=SA+Hale